AN EIGHTEENTH-CENTURY
GARLAND

An arrangement for the winter season

AN EIGHTEENTH-CENTURY GARLAND

THE FLOWER AND FRUIT ARRANGEMENTS
OF COLONIAL WILLIAMSBURG

BY LOUISE B. FISHER

COLONIAL WILLIAMSBURG

Williamsburg, Virginia

1951

Photographs by Thomas L. Williams

IN MEMORY OF
JOHN ROBERTS FISHER

Foreword

OUR clipper ships, and others before them, touched many a Far East port, bringing back exotic cargoes. It is not recorded, however, that among them were included those rules of Chinese and Japanese flower arrangement which have now become so strict an orthodoxy among bouquet-makers. So it is a relief to read Mrs. Fisher's account of the flower arrangements she makes, which are among the glories of Williamsburg, and to find no rules or solemn directives. In a manner as ingenuous as her bouquets, she tells what she uses and why. Behind them are the custom and authority of the past, and she knows the past well. In a sense her arrangements are glorified tussie-mussies, those tenderly conceived and simply combined hand bouquets of an older generation, and they serve an admirably humanizing purpose. Flowers and people are closely allied—living flesh responds to living flowers. We can well imagine the Governor and his lady coming downstairs in the Palace of a morning, their eyes quickened by the flowers there. The day starts right. Whatever duties lie ahead lose some of their bothersome injunctions.

To the curious gardener, Mrs. Fisher re-introduces many old friends among early American plant explorers: Peter Collinson and those English eighteenth-century gentleman botanists who sent forth our earliest plant hunters. Gardens of England were made richer by their finds, which English housewives found "pretty" to combine in a container. Just so, Mrs. Fisher searches the meadows and roadsides of Tidewater Virginia for wildings and brings back many an unlikely branch to crown a vase. The list of what she grows at Williamsburg for her arrangements might well serve as a guide to beginning gardeners. They are obviously "period" flowers, but it is not at all a bad idea to garden within an arc of years.

Thanks to sound scholarship, Mrs. Fisher has been able to lay a few legends by the heels, notably that about the Scotch broom growing around Yorktown. It did not spring from Cornwallis' horse fodder, but appears to have been flourishing there before the lines of battle were drawn.

Mrs. Fisher has a unique setting for her art. Mr. John D. Rockefeller, Jr., in giving reality to the Reverend Dr. William A. R. Goodwin's dream of the restoration of the colonial capital of Virginia, conceived of the project not as a dusty museum but as a living town. It is fitting that in the exhibition buildings at Williamsburg Mrs. Fisher should combine fidelity to the past with the freshness of flowers.

"An Eighteenth-Century Garland" is a valuable addition to any garden library. It will be treasured and often used. Under its influence, one may hope that the influence of Williamsburg will be revealed in our flower shows. How welcome these artless arrangements would be amid the clutter of self-conscious, macabre combinations of plant material so often be-medaled today.

RICHARDSON WRIGHT

West Chatham, Massachusetts
September, 1950

Acknowledgments

ALTHOUGH I would like to be able to acknowledge all the help I have received since I first started work for Colonial Williamsburg, I can take space only to express my appreciation to a few individuals for their share in making this book possible. I am most grateful to Mrs. Helen Bullock for her encouragement and assistance in research. Alden Hopkins, Resident Landscape Architect of Colonial Williamsburg, J. B. Brouwers, under whose supervision the cutting garden was developed, and Alden Eaton, under whom it is now maintained, have contributed in many ways, over a long period of time, to the project here described. Dr. E. M. Betts of the University of Virginia checked the manuscript thoroughly and made many valuable suggestions which I have gratefully incorporated.

To Miss Joan Parry I wish to extend special thanks. Her enthusiasm, and her help in preparing the manuscript, were equally indispensable. The photographs are all the work of the Staff Photographer of Colonial Williamsburg; I believe they speak for themselves, and that my debt to the ability and patience of Thomas L. Williams is apparent.

There is another debt of gratitude which goes back to the time before there was a Flower Section. Today I have the help of an assistant, a chauffeur (who is so much more than chauffeur; he does everything but arrange the flowers), and the use of a station wagon. But in the beginning I did the flower work alone and in addition to my duties as a hostess. Had it not been for the untiring help of my husband, who gave unsparingly of his time, I would never have succeeded, and would have had no story to tell in this book.

L. B. F.

Williamsburg, Virginia
October 26, 1950

Contents

Illustrations

AN EIGHTEENTH-CENTURY
GARLAND

I. Discoveries and Rewards

ANY gardener who prefers to be out weeding and planting rather than working indoors will I know agree with me that the hardest part of moving to a new home is leaving the garden behind. When in 1930 my husband and I first came to Williamsburg (where he was to be the head of the Department of Languages of the College of William and Mary), my chief concern was to bring with me as much of my small garden in Ashland, Virginia, as I could possibly contrive to do. I remember our neighbors' amused astonishment when we arrived with one truck of furniture and two trucks of flowers.

In those days the work of restoring Williamsburg to its eighteenth-century appearance had only begun. Electric light poles and wires still marred the Duke of Gloucester Street, construction was in progress on every hand, and of the seven exhibition buildings now open to the public, only the Raleigh Tavern had been completed.

The Raleigh opened in the fall of 1932 and early in the following spring I accepted a position as hostess there. To give the building a natural, lived-in appearance, flowers were arranged in several of the rooms. I had not been at my new duties long when I was asked to take over the responsibility for these arrangements. The assignment was a welcome one and for materials I drew heavily on my own and other private gardens.

It was not until visitors questioned the use of certain plant materials that I realized the arrangements should include only those wild and cultivated flowers that were available in the eighteenth century. It came as a surprise when I was asked why we were using grapefruit in a colonial setting when the fruit was unknown to the colonists. And how, I was asked, could I justify the use of dahlias? Questions such as these not only aroused my curiosity but became a challenge. The busy Research Department was only too glad to hand over the problem of authenticity to me, and gradually not only the responsibility for the arrangements, but also the question of which flowers could properly be included in them, became mine. What had started as a hobby was soon a full-time job.

The amount of plant material needed for the flower decorations created an urgent need for a cutting garden where quantities of flowers could be grown and where I could gather liberally without fear of despoiling the appearance of the restored gardens. This cutting garden was soon flourishing. Today, over two hundred kinds of annuals, perennials, bulbs, and shrubs are at my disposal. In addition I draw heavily on the wild native plants.

I must hasten to add that for the most part our native flowers are gathered from a large tract of woods belonging to Colonial Williamsburg, the same tract from which trees and shrubs were transplanted to the Palace and other gardens when the restoration work first started. With these woods so close at hand, it seemed easier in most cases to gather wildings there rather than to take space in the cutting garden which otherwise could be devoted to garden flowers.

I should also like to explain why it is not possible to grow the identical variety of each flower that was grown in the eighteenth century. I discovered in my research that the craze for the landscape garden which swept Europe in the latter part of that century was responsible for the total disappearance of many original varieties. At a time when attention was focused on design rather than on plant material, many flowers were banished into inconspicuous corners to make way for the wide vistas demanded by the prevailing fashion. The result was twofold: not only were some plants lost altogether to cultivation, but some that today we think of as new varieties—the double nasturtium, for instance, the parrot tulip, and the double larkspur—were actually grown in the eighteenth century. Today we can grow only modern varieties of these old plants, but we choose varieties which we believe most nearly resemble the flowers cultivated in colonial days.

With my cutting garden established and the wild garden of the fields and woods to draw on, I turned my attention to the problem of authentic containers. Since these were recognized as integral furnishings of the buildings, we were able to acquire actual antiques in great variety. This is important, for my choice of flowers depends not only on their setting but also on the container I intend to use.

The collection includes vases and bowls of china, pottery, pewter, brass, and alabaster; wooden cups, a glass goblet, and such curious specialties as "bricks" and fingered posy holders.

My favorites, the English delft "bricks," are so unusual that perhaps I should take a moment to describe them. We have three pairs, of which two are oblong in shape, the third square. What makes them unique is that instead of having the usual open top the bricks are enclosed. Small round holes around a larger hole in the center pierce the top and give admirable support to the flower stems. One pair has a lovely boat and river view design in blue, another is decorated in attractive soft blue and henna tones, and the third, the square-shaped set, has brownish-lavender shades, especially useful in tying in with the colors in the Palace bedroom above the little dining room.

The fingered posy holders are also among my curious containers. One, a white, five-fingered posy holder, is customarily used in the Wythe House. A nine-fingered holder, by its peculiar shade of blue and its ducks'-head handles, shows the Chinese influence in eighteenth-century containers. It is not easy to arrange flowers in this holder but the results can be most rewarding.

A brass Monteith I use has interest as well as beauty. Named for its designer, it was intended originally as a punch bowl and the decoration around the upper edge served both as ornament and as a place to hang the punch cups. There is also a two-handled rummer of brass.

Other bowls include a fine one in blue and white Worcester china, a small one in pewter, and another in Lowestoft. I would include among the most useful and satisfactory containers in the collection an old Worcester soup tureen; flowers rarely fail to look particularly happy in almost all tureens.

A delft urn, two blue and white Chinese temple jars, three small bud vases, and a fan-shaped vase all have their turn. I frequently use a tall Dutch delft vase dating from about 1690 which is a special treasure, and also a two-handled Bristol delft vase similar to those appearing in the Furber prints and most satisfactory and pleasing for arrangements.

For potted plants I use a Lowestoft jardiniere of oriental baroque style, two jardinieres in Wedgwood creamware and one in porcelain.

Preparing an arrangement in the West Hall of the Governor's Palace

Robert Furber's flower print for April

Two cups of spiral-turned elm I use only for the dried bouquets in winter, which gives them a special and delightful use.

Lastly there are teardrop vases, in small, medium, and tall sizes. These, together with a big glass goblet, are reproductions. I use the teardrop vases and an original garniture set in delft for the sideboards and mantels in the Palace Dining Room. The teardrop vases in two sizes, the five-fingered posy holder, and the square bricks are all available in modern reproductions and are a joy to anyone who has fallen under the spell of making arrangements in the eighteenth-century manner. But the bricks, especially, are very attractive for any type of arrangement.

When I first started to use the old containers I felt the heavy responsibility of working daily with irreplaceable, breakable antiques, many of them over two hundred years old. Now, however, I feel only pleasure in handling such treasures and have become accustomed to their everyday use. Casualties have fortunately been rare, and in only one instance was damage done that was past repairing.

The establishment of a cutting garden and the search for contemporary containers was simple compared with the search for descriptions of eighteenth-century flower arrangements. I turned first to the old garden books by men such as Philip Miller and John Hill, to the travel diaries of explorers such as John Bartram and Peter Kalm, and to the letters and diaries of Thomas Jefferson, William Byrd, and John Custis in Virginia and Peter Collinson in London. They became my friends, and in the last chapter of this book I will tell a little of the great part they played in garden history.

There is no lack of evidence that the colonists loved to use both wild and cultivated flowers for decorations. As Peter Kalm wrote in his *Travels into North America*, "The *English* ladies were used to gather great quantities of . . . *Life everlasting*, and to pluck them with the stalks. For they put them into pots with or without water, amongst other fine flowers which they had gathered both in the gardens and in the fields, and placed them as an ornament in the rooms. The *English* ladies in general are much inclined to have fine flowers all the summer long, in or upon the chimneys, sometimes upon a table, or before the windows, either on account of their fine appearance, or for the sake of their sweet scent."

Details of the composition of these arrangements, however, were all too sparse. Fortunately another source was available in contemporary illustrations. These often show small vases and bowls of flowers and fruits as well as potted plants. Sheraton's furniture book, too, shows small bowls of flowers on several sideboards—"Basons, or Flower-pots" as Philip Miller called them. But it was from the large flower prints and paintings that I obtained the best information.

Seventeenth-century plant illustration in England in no way compared with the famous flower-piece paintings of continental artists, particularly those of the Dutch school. English illustrators were more concerned with accuracy than with beauty in their drawings of fruits and flowers. During the eighteenth century, however, many beautiful prints were produced in England. No longer purely documentary, the English prints of this period were also imaginative portrayals, and since artist as well as botanist contributed to them, they have been as valuable in serving as guides for arrangements as they have been for identifying flowers and fruits of the period.

It is to Robert Furber, a Kensington nurseryman, that we are most indebted. He issued in 1730 a catalogue which he named *Twelve Months of Flowers*. The flowers are botanically accurate and arranged according to the month in which they bloom, there being twelve large engravings, one for each month of the year. Moreover, every flower is numbered and at the bottom of the page its name is engraved, so that the whole forms a treasured key to the popular English flowers, among them American flowers that had been introduced at an earlier period. A set of these Furber prints may be seen on the staircase wall in the George Wythe House. They are used more than any others as models for the arrangements in the buildings of Colonial Williamsburg.

Although we had Peter Kalm's word that the English ladies in the colonies gathered great bunches of life everlasting to place "amongst other fine flowers," and Philip Miller, in his *Dictionary*, frequently ends a description with the remark that the flowers look well with other flowers in halls or in front of fireplaces, I was troubled because these quotations were our only assurance that the large "printy" bouquets were actually stylish in the eighteenth century. The illustrations of arrangements in the Sheraton furniture book and in the many contemporary interior paintings that show flowers on tables and sideboards were only suitable for small vases, and usually featured a single type of flower rather than the generous mixtures of the prints. It was not until 1946 that confirming visual evidence was finally discovered. At that time, two early eighteenth-century portraits, one painted in Virginia, the other in Maryland, were brought to my attention. In each painting a little girl is shown standing beside a table on which rests a large bouquet unmistakably arranged in the style of the prints!

I must explain my phrase "printy" bouquets. I deliberately use this word to describe the affinity of my arrangements to the prints of the period but it must not be assumed that the arrangements are exact copies. What I have tried to do is to capture as far as possible the feeling and style of the artists' interpretations, for even if I were presumptuous enough to attempt literal copies, the trial would be doomed to failure: some prints show all the flowers that bloom in a whole month, others show flowers that bloom at different seasons. Even with a greenhouse to draw on it would not be possible to have all the flowers appearing in any one print fit for cutting on the same day. Consequently, although real effort is made to capture the quality of the prints, or, as we have become accustomed to express it, to make the arrangements look as printy as possible, we do not attempt to duplicate our models.

Most of the prints use a great many flowers. I experimented first with flat bouquets, without filling in the sides or backs. I soon found this method quite inadequate. The arrangements had to be fuller because a bouquet designed for real use is viewed from the sides as well as from the front, and so must have more than just a "face."

Perhaps I should say here that I use one accessory only in my work. It is a heavy criss-cross square flower holder for shallow bowls which enables me to keep the flowers in place until the basic shape is outlined and I am ready to fill in the whole. Not only do I think it unlikely that the putty, string, wire, and weights frequently used in flower decorations today were known in the eighteenth century, but I simply do not have the temperament to work with them.

In making my arrangements I first outline the desired shape with dwarf and tall branching flowers and with whatever foliage is used.

Posy holders, bricks, and bowls from the Palace collection

Miscellaneous containers used in the Palace arrangements

When the framework is complete I select one kind of flower, filling in from the top to the bottom of the container, making various lines as I work. Sometimes, as an alternative, I work with one color, using different materials. By this method I can retain the beautiful curves that are natural to the material. Once I have the desired effect I mass the more solid flowers just over the top of the container, fill in the sides and back, and the arrangement is then ready for its setting. This method of composition is clearly indicated in eighteenth-century prints.

The choice of flowers depends on the room for which they are intended. Light-colored flowers look best against dark wall-hangings or dark woodwork, deeper toned flowers against a light background. Similarly, quality or texture is important. Coarser flowers are better suited for a large room such as the Upper Middle Room in the Palace, the more delicate blooms for a small one such as the Parlor.

It is the general policy of Colonial Williamsburg that decorations throughout the exhibition buildings be used with restraint, so that the rooms have a lived-in appearance rather than an air of being ready for some festivity. This, I believe, is how most people really like best to see flowers arranged. But the bouquets themselves are usually very full, especially those in the large rooms. "Buxom bouquets," Mr. Richardson Wright once called them, a description that, like the word "printy," has now become common parlance in our Williamsburg flower language. And there is also the expression "just one more." To explain this I must admit to a personal foible. I delight in these arrangements, for not only am I fond of using a lot of flowers, but I find it hard to resist the impulse to add "just one more." So this phrase too has long since become a byword among my associates.

At first I acted on the assumption that flowers were placed on dining tables as ornaments, but no evidence was forthcoming to confirm this idea. I did find, however, that meat and poultry were frequently used as centerpieces, relics presumably of the custom of earlier days when everything on the overloaded table was intended to be part of the meal. The word "dormants," by which these centerpieces were known, signifies that they were intended for decoration as well as food, and were thus forerunners of flower arrangements on dining tables today, when less hearty appetites make room for elegance. It was therefore decided to arrange only fruit and nuts on the dining-room tables until evidence was found of flowers being used for this purpose.

In those days the housewife could afford to be generous with fruit and nuts. Apples, pears, peaches, persimmons, pomegranates, figs, apricots, grapes, cherries all flourished in Virginia, and from the West Indies lemons, limes, and pineapples were occasionally available. There were many native nuts such as the chestnut, as well as introductions, among them the almond and English walnut. Catesby recalls seeing pomegranates growing in great perfection in the gardens of William Byrd, and from Byrd's *Secret Diary* we know that he once sent "four great pomegranates" to the governor in Williamsburg. On many other occasions he gave the governor cherries. Byrd mentions among twenty-five varieties of apples, seven that "one can preserve all year long," and of twenty-nine sorts of pears, six that would last all winter.

There were ways by which fruit could be assured throughout the year. In England apples and pears were packed between layers of dry moss in jars that were sealed with rosin to keep them air tight. Then the whole was covered with sand. Grapes were preserved in ashes.

Fruit was also forced to ripen early, out of season, by such devices as forcing under glass or heating hollow brick walls against which fruit trees were trained. Cherries could be ripened in March, apricots and strawberries in April, grapes in May. Certain flowers, too, such as the snapdragon and the rose, were forced in spring. Indeed, in England it was the florist's boast that his wife could decorate her room at pleasure with out-of-season flowers. Thus above all others in the land was she able to share this privilege with the king.

Garden books of the period prove conclusively that dried flowers were used for house decoration during the winter. Commonly called "everlastings," they include pearly everlastings, globe amaranths, and strawflowers. Philip Miller, writing of them in his *Figures of Plants*, says "These Flowers were formerly much more cultivated in the Gardens near *London* than at present; and were brought to the Markets in great Plenty during the Winter Season, to adorn Rooms. The Gardeners had a Method of staining them of a deep red and blue Colour, by dipping them into different Liquids. So they brought them to the Markets in Bunches of four different Colours; white, purple, blue, and red: And when their Stalks were put into Glasses with Sand, the Flowers would continue in Beauty till the Spring." I have not found anything better than sand to hold such light materials properly.

To supplement and as alternatives to the dried flower arrangements I use potted plants as well as the evergreens of pine, cedar, bayberry, magnolia, and holly. It may seem odd that it is possible to include potted plants in the buildings, but we believe a small greenhouse existed in the Palace garden and presumably they were raised there. We do know from the "Garden Notes" of Lady Skipwith, wife of Sir Peyton

Skipwith of Mecklenburg County, that she used both cyclamen and lantana.

So, after we have moved through the months of fresh flowers to harvest, we come to Christmas. The Williamsburg Christmas decorations are based on the evidence of English customs and those found in Virginia records. Not only do I decorate the mantels and window seats in addition to the usual dried flower or evergreen arrangements throughout the Palace and Wythe House, but every dining table also has a special arrangement of fruits and nuts and evergreens. At every window hangs a wreath, lit by candlelight at night, and balconies, wrought-iron gates, and doors are festooned with garlands of evergreens.

Much has been said about our eighteenth-century manner of flower arranging, and about our efforts to make the decoration as authentic as possible. In one respect I certainly have not strayed; I feel sure that one of the most authentic features of the arrangements is the physical environment in which they are made. There are no conveniences at the Palace. Therefore I find myself in the narrow West Hall with a long marble-top table on which to work, a sheet spread on the floor to catch the discarded flowers and broken stems, every inch of floor space, except where I am standing, filled a foot high with the dear departed bouquets. On the steps outside are the several buckets of flowers to be used, as well as those filled with water for washing and filling the containers. When it is raining, windy, or very hot—and it is one of these many days in the year—all these buckets have to be brought inside, and I am completely surrounded by dead flowers, and the many buckets. And so there is one thing I can say with complete assurance: this method of flower arranging is definitely *in the eighteenth-century manner*.

II. The Spring of the Year

SPRING usually comes no earlier to the Virginia Tidewater than its official date in March, and it is not until this month that I replace the dried bouquets with the first fresh flowers. So begins another year of flower and fruit decoration.

Throughout March the arrangements are of necessity simple because there is not a wide choice of material. Indeed this is the one time of year when I supplement our own supply by buying from a florist snapdragons, larkspur, stock, carnations, Madonna lilies, Spanish iris, and tulips. We allow ourselves this leeway on the assumption that some early flowers and a few potted plants were raised in the greenhouse on the Palace grounds, but I use them sparingly, for one or at most two arrangements in the Palace.

Daffodils, wherever they are grown, are greeted as harbingers of spring. I think of all the spring flowers we give to them our warmest welcome, grateful after winter for their cheerful freshness. Here in Williamsburg they take pride of place not only in our early spring arrangements but also in our hearts. It is not, I think, merely a whim of fancy to believe that many of the daffodils that bloom each year in Williamsburg gardens are direct descendants of those bulbs the first women colonists brought with them to remind them of home.

Narcissi were introduced early in the colonies and then, as now, there were times of confusion over the names of the many varieties. Narcissus, the common daffodil or Lent lily, was well known. There was the slender jonquil with the narrow rushlike leaves and fragrant flower, *Narcissus jonquilla.* Another, the poet's narcissus, *Narcissus poeticus,* the lovely strong-growing flower with a red-margined corona from which it gets the name pheasant's eye, was the flower of flowers of Greek and Roman verse, the first flower that Theocritus placed in his *Europas Garland.* The double white variety was the daffodil that caused an altercation between Collinson, who called it the sweet white narcissus, and Bartram, who called it the double sweet daffodil.

The cornelian cherry, companion to the daffodil, is a welcome addition now. Its yellow-laden branches mix well with daffodils, adding a touch of lightness to the stiff-stemmed flowers. It ties in well also with the plum blossoms that open toward the end of March. These flower sprays are lovely either by themselves or mixed with other flowers.

I am aware that few prints show the use of sprays of fruit blossoms in decoration, but it is reasonable to assume that peach, pear, and apple branches were all brought into the house in their season.

The shrubs and trees give us our warmest color tones during spring. The red and yellow maple blossoms look well together in tall vases; the soft gray pussy willow is always highly decorative alone and, like the cornelian cherry, has the added advantage of being a "good mixer."

Green foliage is, of course, the best of all good mixers and invariably is a tremendous help in tying together mixed colors in a vase or in a room. If the winter has not been too severe, March is the month when the magnolia leaves wear their richest gloss, appearing highly polished. Branches of these leaves in tall vases make a pleasing contrast in a room where spring's paler delicacies are arranged, and I make good use of them.

Hyacinths are universal favorites and last well indoors. They are, as John Hill pointed out, natives of the East, children of the sun; and if there is a certain pensive quality both in their name and color, it finds full compensation in their exotic scent. House warmth will draw this from them until their fragrance pervades the whole room.

I use both single and double hyacinths and find the English delft bricks ideal for their arrangement, as they are for almost all the flowering bulbs. Short, heavy-headed flowers are never easy to handle. Anyone who has once used these bricks will, I am sure, never be without them. In the large oval opening at the center of the brick I almost always use some kind of foliage to keep the flowers in place, but the smaller holes give all the support the flowers need to stand alone. Moreover, these bricks are the only containers I know that will hold and "still" a daffodil exactly as I place it, and everyone who has arranged them knows how they delight to turn their heads in exactly the opposite direction from that intended. Hyacinths and narcissi look particularly well together in the bricks.

Snapdragons are flowers I use over a very long period, from the first early forced ones from the florist to the plants we raise in the cutting garden. They are among the most decorative and useful flowers and have long been beloved of florists for their long blooming season, and by decorators for their lasting quality. In the eighteenth century they were known in white, red, and yellow, plain and variegated forms, and were used both as pot plants and cut flowers. I use them constantly.

The whole tempo of the flowering world quickens as the year turns into April, and it is April which provides us with the fullest basket of true spring flowers as well as the first flood of flowering trees and shrubs. Hyacinths and daffodils still linger and mingle with the crowd of cowslips, scillas, wallflowers, columbines, and other old-time favorites.

Cowslips in a blue Wedgwood bowl; cowslips mixed with the porcelain-blue scillas; cowslips and wallflowers, a head of honeyed sweetness—these everyone loves, and to my mind they are the freshest flowers of all.

Grape hyacinths, both the common and the feathered varieties, provide us with another lovely blue to mix in with the predominant yellows of spring. Thomas Jefferson noted in his *Garden Book* the feathered grape hyacinth, and no doubt the ones now growing at Monticello are descendants of those Jefferson brought from his early home at Shadwell.

Pansies, short-stemmed at first, are not easy to arrange. Later I can use them as fillers, picking a whole cluster and using them at the base of a brick arrangement.

The atamasco lily, native to Virginia and other Southern states, is not only one of April's treasures but also one of my special favorites. The Jamestown lily, as it is known locally, grows abundantly on Jamestown Island. I think of Mark Catesby, the English botanist, when I gather these white blooms; he too found them growing here and noted that they were as numerous as the field cowslips and wild orchids in his native fields of England. I think, too, of Collinson's lovely, terse description when he wrote to Bartram: "Thee sent me what we call the Atamasco Lily, from its shape. It has a blush of purple before the flow-

Tulips and camass among glossy magnolia leaves

er opens; is white within. It is properly a *Lilio-Narciss:* the leaves of the last, and flower of the first. If, in thy rambles, thee happens on this flower, pray send a root or two."

The stately crown imperial, as its name suggests, is one of April's prides. Once it had a place in the cutting garden, even though it is hard to establish. But it was banished because the hostesses in the exhibition buildings found it an intolerably evil-smelling companion. No arrangement, however, gives a more printy effect than one of spring flowers crowned by this imperial lily in both its orange and its yellow varieties.

April brings us the redbud, the lilac, and the white and pink flowering dogwood. The dogwood is beautiful not only in spring but throughout the year. The green leaves turning red in the fall are especially good for pressing, the horizontal branches being excellent in winter decoration. The red fruit berries are also attractive, and so are the small gray buds of next year's bloom tipping each branch.

There are few places in America where the native redbud blooms more beautifully than in Virginia. As might be imagined, an air of mystery has always surrounded its common name, Judas tree. I prefer the name by which the Spanish know it—the love tree, on account, no doubt, of its heart-shaped leaves. But call it what we may, it adapts itself particularly well both in arrangements on its own and in combination with other shrubs, especially the lilac.

The lilac is an adaptable immigrant from Europe and Asia which can make a home for itself in every country. So in every heart it quickly becomes established as an old-time favorite. We know of the lilacs John Custis grew here in Williamsburg in the 1730's, and it is not fanciful to imagine that lilacs adorned many a Williamsburg room in those eighteenth-century Aprils that do not seem to us so very long ago.

I especially enjoy arranging a bowl of white and lilac-colored lilacs with pale pink snapdragons under the portrait of Charles II's queen, Catherine of Braganza, in the Ballroom of the Palace. There is between that half-smiling, half-disdainful face and the cool, impersonal flower a curious affinity I find impossible to explain in words.

Spring and summer meet in May, the late spring flowers claiming equal place with those of early summer. What a host they are: lupine and larkspur, dame's rocket and Canterbury bell; single and double Oriental poppies; red and white valerian and speedwell; pinks, peonies, daisies, sweet peas, iris, and false indigo; feverfew and meadow rue; snapdragon, sweet William, and the humble white candytuft. These are all favorites.

Most of the old garden lists of this country include the sweet William. Like the snapdragon, it was used not only in bouquets but "being planted in Pots," was considered to be "very proper to adorn Court-Yards" at the time of its flowering. Because sweet William possesses a lasting quality and a variety of color, I find it especially valuable in mixed bouquets, and I like to use it particularly with false indigo, pink and white Canterbury bells, poppies, and the golden ragwort.

Yellow is a color that grows less prominent as spring advances, but it is a color I introduce whenever possible into my mixed bouquets. Golden ragwort and leopard bane both give a useful yellow touch at this time of year.

White flowering candytuft, which is effective either in small Chinese bud vases or in mixed bunches, has the freshness of printed cotton, a quality it shares with Canterbury bells. Another campanula, the chimney flower, enjoyed great popularity during the eighteenth century, and was described as being commonly cultivated to adorn chimneys and halls during the summer season. The recommendation was also made that the chimney flower be spread flat against sticks, espalierwise, so that, fan-shaped, it would cover a fireplace.

Peonies were much-prized introductions from England, where that prolific author John Hill complained they were ignored for no other reason than the old truth which says familiarity breeds contempt. "There is not a Flower more known than this in the *English* Gardens, and scarce one so specious. It is too common to be much regarded: but this is a false Taste: if new brought from *America*, the whole Botanic World would resound with its Praise." This gives an interesting sidelight on the eagerness with which eighteenth-century Europe welcomed every new plant from North America, even the skunk cabbage.

Larkspur has always been a favorite both in beds and cutting gardens, and in the eighteenth century both the single and double varieties were widely grown in many colors. Larkspurs and snapdragons are lovely arranged in a Chinese vase, and lupines and larkspurs are particularly happy together in a delft vase; so are double white larkspurs, lupines, and marsh marigolds. The marigolds, which last well, I gather beside the lake in the Palace Gardens.

Amsonia, which is rarely seen today, is a choice plant, though it is not showy, and makes a welcome addition both to the flower border and to a mixed arrangement. Its terminal panicles of starlike, gray-blue flowers never fail to bring forth favorable comment and questions as to its name and habitat.

Monkshood, another blue-toned flower, was so called for its resemblance to a friar's cowl, Miller tells us. It was popular, like the chimney flower, "to furnish Flower-pots for Chimneys" and was grown in England by eighteenth-century florists for the May market.

Eighteenth-century gardeners loved sweet peas although they did not know them in the incredible range of color and variety grown today. I like to place them in one of the blue delft bricks, where they look fresh and attractive. Blue is a color that harmonizes with them particularly well and you will find sweet peas and blue sage extremely pretty together. Surprisingly, for so light a flower, you will also find that sweet peas can be mixed in with larger bouquets. Sometimes I have used them in this way effectively with meadow rue, with Canterbury bells, the wild golden ragwort, coreopsis, and English daisies. They are a handsome company set in the Worcester tureen.

With the exception of the lily and the rose, the iris is probably more often seen in early tapestries than any other flower. Because irises are special favorites of mine and bloom in variety over a long period, I use them constantly. The yellow, blue, white, and purple German iris, and the Spanish iris in the same colors, are the varieties I use most frequently. They are among the most adaptable flowers to arrange and I love to mix them with columbines—excellent company for each other in house or garden. Blue iris, dwarf red horse chestnut, sweet peas, and yellowwood; blue iris, poppies and peonies, spirea, and meadow rue; indeed with almost every flower this poor man's orchid, as the iris is sometimes called, looks well. And I should add that meadow rue, though so delicate in appearance, lasts well and has far greater stamina than many of the more robust-looking flowers.

A very full spring bouquet in which bright red tulips and carnations are handsomely set
off by dogwood and daffodil, lilac and stock

But it is for the tulip that Charles Evelyn reserved the title "the glory of the spring." Ever since its introduction to Europe from Constantinople and the Levant the tulip has held its place as *the* florists' flower, and when it reached Holland in the early part of the seventeenth century it took that country by storm. Rich and poor alike gambled on the bulb as Wall Street might gamble on stocks and bonds. When the day of reckoning came, Holland woke up to find the once rare tulip covering the flat fenland like some great multi-colored patchwork quilt. Fortunes that had been made overnight were as quickly lost. Tulipomania left its mark.

The Keizerskroon tulips and other early varieties are with us in Williamsburg by April, followed by the more ornate and fantastic parrot tulips. Beautiful in vases by themselves or with other flowers, they look well, I might say, almost anywhere and everywhere. I use them often in the nine-fingered posy holder, in Chinese vases, and in the old English bricks.

I never fail to make at least one arrangement of the tulip Gala Beauty and our native coral honeysuckle. Gala Beauty is a superb cottage tulip, a rich golden yellow, feathered and splashed with scarlet. These flowers in one of the old bricks are ideal for the Lower Hall in the Wythe House, where they pick up the faded henna red in the hall rug and in the coverings of the chair seats. They are appropriate, too, in the large bedroom of the Palace where the colors in the carpet and fire screen are much the same. Yet not for color alone is this arrangement pleasing; there is, in the graceful curve of the tulip and the winding spray of the honeysuckle, a perfection of contrast that gives an especially supple quality to the combination.

May brings such a wealth of all kinds of flowers that we are apt to ignore the flowering shrubs and trees. If we do, it is our loss. Even with such superabundance it is a mistake not to use these lovely sprays, especially when we find among them almost every color. Any one alone is lovely; mixed with other flowers they are superb, and, since I like generous buxom bouquets, I use a quantity of flowering branches in my arrangements.

Pink to red we find in the red horse chestnut, the smokebush, the English hawthorn, the mountain laurel, Tatarian honeysuckle, and native spirea. The native wisteria echoes in May the cool, contrasting tones of April's lilac. Wild senna, St. John's wort, and Scotch broom give orange and yellow tones, and sweet shrub gives brown.

White, which April gave us in the dogwood and the fruit blossom, we find in May in the mock orange, ideal for all-white arrangements; in New Jersey tea, fringe tree, and yellowwood with its lovely long racemes of white and fragrant pea-like flowers resembling the laburnum; in silver bell, hydrangea, native white spirea, sorrel, the magnolia, the black haw viburnum, and snowball bush.

Stewartia, which blooms in June, I consider one of the most beautiful of all flowers. Though it lasts but a few hours after picking, I cannot resist the trouble of making one arrangement even if it will be gone by nightfall.

New Jersey tea, once used as a substitute for tea, is very decorative and worthy of wider recognition both in the garden and in arrangements. Yellowwood is perfect in mixed bouquets. The tea shrub (not to be confused with New Jersey tea), although it does not flower at this time, is yet valuable for the beauty and long-lasting quality of its leaves. You can discover for yourself how versatile these leaves can be by using them either in large mixed bouquets or in small containers, such as the bricks, where I like to mix them with small flowers like the little bright-orange French marigolds.

Highbush cranberry, blooming now, is generous: not only does the flower blend happily in a bowl of columbines, or in a combination of late double white daffodils, irises, and snapdragons, and even a few red roses, but its late summer-autumn fruit is highly useful and decorative.

White and green are probably the safest colors to use in any room: they never fail to tone in satisfactorily with the most difficult colors in furnishings, particularly where simplicity is the keynote, as in the Wythe House. This was a private home, a gentleman's town house where today flowers are used in the Parlor, the halls, the Study, and in some of the bedrooms. In the Parlor, which has green curtains, a needlework carpet, and a sofa almost cerise in tone, the colors have to be chosen with care. The container usually selected is the white Wedgwood five-fingered posy holder. Of course, an all-white arrangement is eminently suitable, but a mixed bouquet can be used if one is careful of the pink and red tones. Green foliage also helps to tie in the mixed colors with this room. Nothing looks better in the Lower Hall than coral honeysuckle or the blossoms of the red horse chestnut, these colors blending well with the soft, old rosy-henna shades. In one of the bedrooms, a touch of purple is introduced whenever possible to pick up the purple color of the knitting which lies on an occasional table. The knitting is only one of many similar homely touches in the exhibition buildings: surely the mistress of the house was there only a moment before?

We might well, with but a handful of our own native shrubs, count ourselves rich indeed. Even the entranced Collinson, who was essentially a prose writer and not a poet, used the word "ecstasy" when he confessed to Bartram that, seeing the mountain laurel, the fringe tree, and the allspice of Carolina bloom together, he was overcome with their beauty.

Bartram's "double sweet daffodil" in a square delft brick

Lilac, a good mixer, also beautiful alone

Snowballs, narcissi, poppy anemones, budding irises, and camass in the delft urn

Gala Beauty tulips and coral honeysuckle in a delft brick

Late spring and early summer flowers, among them amsonia and highbush cranberry

Snapdragons and iris in the five-fingered posy holder

A summer bunch with hollyhock and Yorktown onion

Queen Anne's lace

III. High Pomp of Summer

———————————————————————————————

JUNE is a riotous month bringing in its train the late spring flowers: the cornflowers and columbines, the pinks and daisies, dame's rocket and iris; the pollen-dusted snapdragon; cotton-fresh candytuft among the silks of annual and Oriental poppies; speedwell and valerian. Above all, June is the month of the lily and the rose. These, with a host of others, make high pomp of summer.

The most colorful time of all, it is also, for the flower decorator, the most exacting. These summer months I am about my business early. The cutting and care of flowers is now more than ever demanding. Gathering my flowers as soon after sunrise as possible, I keep them in a dark, cool basement until I need them the following morning. Six or eight hours is as long as most flowers require to recuperate from cutting, and I leave them twenty-four hours only because it best suits the timetable I set for my work.

I have learned to cut only half-opened flowers. Phlox particularly I like to gather just as the petals begin to loosen. Others, such as peonies, wild senna, and all fruit blossoms, I cut while they are still close in the bud.

Now wild flowers are also among my staunch reliables. Indeed one of my greatest pleasures has been my own discovery of the wild flowers of Virginia. I had no idea there was such a wealth of beautiful native material. It is curious that our wild flowers seem always to have attracted more attention in Europe than in their native North America. Mac-Mahon, in his *American Gardener's Calendar* published in 1806, asks why we Americans neglect our native plants instead of cultivating and improving them. He points out that in Europe plants are not rejected because they are indigenous, but are valued as highly as species imported from abroad.

This is the season for turtlehead, Cupid's dart, coreopsis, and the long racemes of the yellow, pea-like thermopsis flowers which resemble false indigo. It is also the season of calendulas and both French and African marigolds. Although the marigolds do not recommend themselves for their smell, nevertheless they give generously the yellow and orange tones typical of summer and fall decorations. There are, too, both the blue lobelia and the red lobelia (commonly called the cardinal flower), beard tongue, and summer phlox. Phlox was a great favorite in England, John Hill remarking that although it was regarded in North America as "an elegant Weed; with us it is deservedly raised to the Condition of a Garden Plant."

Both the mauve wild bergamot bee balm and the red Oswego bee balm or red bergamot "demand a Place" in every garden, to use Hill's phrase. Loved for the aromatic fragrance of their crushed leaves and for their color, they are valuable for their good neighborliness and are excellent companions in any mixed arrangement.

Summer phlox, cut-and-come-again sunflower, the feathery red prince's plume or, as it is often called, prince's feather, and the white, starlike native clematis make a lovely bunch. All are garden plants. Others that I value highly as cut flowers still remain beyond the garden gate. Of these Queen Anne's lace is indispensable; indeed, I wonder what I should do without it, for it is a perfect mixer in almost every and any summer arrangement.

I am often asked how I manage to keep this plant from wilting. I am sure the secret is in allowing it to remain, when first picked, for from six to eight hours in water in a cool, dark place. This gives the slender stems time to recover and they reward me by standing erect without any trouble after I have arranged them.

Butterfly weed is rampant around Williamsburg and I use it freely because the bright orange flowers are very showy in mixed arrangements. For instance the combination of butterfly weed with wild senna and yellow and orange day lilies makes a decorative and handsome arrangement in the brass Monteith in the Upper Middle Room at the Palace. The colors stand out strikingly and yet blend well with the gold motif of this room given by the wall brackets, the gilt tables and looking glasses, and the hand-tooled leather on the walls that in certain lights is a copper gold and in others a silvered beige. Another much appreciated arrangement is one of statice or sea lavender, Queen Anne's lace, and artemisia. And very effective it is too.

Other wildings that I use constantly are black-eyed Susan, loosestrife, and a variety of grasses. I have a special liking, which I share with the bees, for the sweet clover. When we kept bees my husband would scatter this clover seed along the roadside on his walks so that the bees might give us the particularly good-flavored clover honey.

I remember how I achieved one of my most printy summer effects by an arrangement of the purple-headed Yorktown onion, the flat white heads of yarrow, Queen Anne's lace, and coreopsis with a background of the wild clover. It was especially pleasing in one of the old delft bricks.

Although there is a generous supply of comparatively lasting flowers (and I consider a failure any mixed arrangement that does not last three days), I cannot resist using, either for sentiment or for their beauty, what I call my "timid flowers." My good friend, Fleming Brown, "major-domo" at the Palace, was the first to call these short-lived blooms "timid." Now, like the words "buxom" and "printy," "timid" has become one of our flower colloquialisms.

My timid flowers include the hydrangeas, irises, and day lilies; flowering tobacco, much valued as a pot plant for balconies and shop windows in eighteenth-century London; and the annual and perennial poppies. The Oriental poppy and the large carnation-flowered poppy I value highly not only for their bloom but for their lovely gray-green foliage. By themselves, or in the company of the corn poppies, or in mixed arrangements, they are most effective.

All these I cut the day I use them. Hydrangeas and poppies need special treatment: after stripping the lower foliage, I plunge the cut stems into several inches of boiling water, then transfer them to a cold bath. I cut the stems to the required length beforehand since each time these are broken they must be sealed afresh. And all timid flowers go into an arrangement last so they may be easily renewed.

False indigo, the peach-leaved bellflower, pink annual poppies, white snapdragon, and golden ragwort give me one of the loveliest of summer arrangements. It is a bouquet that is redolent of this season. Another, equally lovely, can be made with thermopsis, Oriental poppies, a few annual poppies, and some of the early goldenrod.

A very full arrangement of early summer flowers

The crape myrtle and the pomegranate are two of our most beautiful shrubs. In thinking of the pomegranate we usually conjure up the lovely red fruit, but the bush is equally valuable for its sprays of bright scarlet, crumpled-petal flowers. Beginning to bloom in June, the flowers continue through the three hot summer months. They retain their color without any fading. The exotic double-flowering variety in particular lends a gay and bold color note in the mixed arrangements.

It is interesting that Miller mentions pomegranate as one of the most valuable flowering trees known in his day. After the Gala Beauty tulips and the yellow irises, it takes its turn with the Oriental poppies in any room in the exhibition buildings where green paint or green curtains and the old wool colors of crewelwork predominate. I have frequently used all these in the Raleigh Tavern.

Crape myrtle, which starts to bloom in July and continues intermittently until October, does not last well, but it is nevertheless extremely valuable. I use it for patching, by which I mean I place it in such a way among long-lasting flowers that I can easily take it out and replace it with a fresh sprig daily. It is by far the most effective pink material I have with which to patch, and I use it a great deal in the Ballroom at the Palace. Apart from its beauty, it is easily handled and can be slipped in and taken out without disturbing the other flowers.

Both crape myrtle and pomegranate are particularly useful because they bloom at a time when few other shrubs are available for use in the Ballroom. Here arrangements are placed on the two rather large tables on either side of the entrance to the Supper Room. Blue Worcester bowls are selected for containers and almost any mixture of colors may be used. In the Ballroom, with its four huge looking glasses on the side walls, hang the portraits of Charles II and George III and their respective queens, Catherine of Braganza and Charlotte of Mecklenburg. In summer old India prints hang at the windows, and the furniture is covered in red and white checked gingham, as listed in an inventory of 1770; in the winter season the curtains are of red damask.

June marks the beginning of another chapter in flower arrangements, for it is now that I make my first journey to the woods to gather both the royal fern and the deliciously scented cinnamon fern. These I take back to the drying room for pressing, the firstcomers to be harvested for winter decoration. I have tried other ferns but have found them unsuccessful because of their tendency to turn a dull brown.

As gardeners must always plan well ahead for all the results they hope for from their gardens, and plant long before they gather, so with the winter decorator. To gather a good harvest of material means making a start now, for it is a six months' harvest, from June to November.

From the garden I start cutting the strawflowers and globe amaranth for winter decoration as soon as June turns into July, and from July onward until frost withers them, I harvest sea lavender, the feathery prince's plume and the more compact cockscomb, Chinese lanterns, as well as the white, the magenta pink, and the yellow yarrows.

I am often asked why I do not use roses more than I do in my decorations. We grow the cabbage rose, the York and Lancaster, the French, the sweetbrier, and the damask, and I do arrange them occasionally. The beauty of pink roses and Madonna lilies in a tall delft vase is well worth the trouble. But generally speaking the old roses do not do well with us and are lacking in the lasting qualities of their modern descendants.

Lilies of all kinds were much esteemed in the colonies and, fittingly enough, our native meadow lily is one of the most suitable of all these for eighteenth-century arrangements. Alone they are always beautiful; with larkspur, the wild Yorktown onion, and the red Oswego bee balm they are superb. No less so the scarlet lily, the American Turk's cap lily, and the old beloved Madonna lily. This last, to my mind, is the most beautiful.

As for carnations, they were ever princes among florists' flowers. Charles Evelyn well said of them that they are the pride of summer. Fanciful in color and design, they have been no less fancifully named: striped, bizarres, rose-leaved flake flowers, July flowers, poet's pink, poet's hyacinth, and even hyacinth of Constantinople. By whatever names they knew them, the colonists loved carnations as we do today, and made every effort to import them in as great variety as possible.

I have mentioned the Yorktown onion but it deserves more than a passing word. It flourishes, probably as a garden escape, along the road from Williamsburg to Yorktown, but we have neither fact nor fiction to tell us the story of its naturalization. Some years ago, a former assistant of mine and her husband saw a number of these mowed down, the stems bending as they withered among the swaths of rank midsummer grass. Gathering all they could, they brought them back to me, exclaiming with excitement "Look, look what we've found." Treasure indeed, lasting treasure too, which we carried to the drying room at the Palace for use in winter decoration.

Later, a kind friend who lived on a side road in the same section, and whose front yard was filled to overflowing with the lovely blooms, generously gave me sufficient bulbs for a good planting in the cutting garden. They have been with us ever since, the flowers becoming not only finer, but of a deeper purple color.

I use these purple heads in fresh arrangements as well as in dried ones. For a room that has as a background certain blues, such as the lead-blue woodwork in the Apollo Room in the Raleigh Tavern, nothing looks better than a group of purple iris or these heavy, purple-headed Yorktown onions, particularly if the color scheme includes a blue bowl, such as the blue delft bowl I used there.

Scotch broom is another highly decorative escape. Since I am often asked about its origin, I would like to mention something of its particularly interesting history. Visitors to the Virginia Peninsula today like the traditional story with which Scotch broom has surrounded itself. It is said that during the Revolution Cornwallis brought forage for his horses to this country and that it contained the seed of Scotch broom. The scattering of the manure set the seed in the ground, where it flourished as we see it today. Yet another version says that the seed was contained in the packing around the cannon balls used by the Redcoats.

In this case, however, fact is stronger than fiction. Several years prior to Cornwallis' stand at Yorktown, Dr. John M. Galt, surgeon and physician of Eastern State Hospital in Williamsburg—the first public mental hospital on this continent—spent some three years in Great Britain and brought back with him to Williamsburg some of the seed. This was in 1767. Writing in 1803 to John H. Cocke, Esq., of Mount Pleasant, he said:

"Dear Sir, When I was at your house you mentioned your Intention of Cultivating the *pride of China* for *feeding sheep*. This will answer for

The fragile native clematis, cool and fresh in the heat of summer

the winter months very well. It did not occur to me then to recommend to your notice the cultivation of *Scotch Broom*, which affords an ample food for between two or three summer months for sheep and Hogs, it affords an abundance of flowers which those animals devour greedily— it fattens them fast & comes early, & will last til the wild fruits are ripe, such as mulberrys, Blackberries & Hurtle berries. . . . When I left England I brought some of the seed that had been gather'd for Twenty-odd years—I planted them as an ornamental flowering shrub in the Garden—they remained in the ground four winters—then Vegetated finely & grew very Luxuriant. . . . In England they have a method of Expediting the Vegetation of Broom—Hawthorn and Holly—by mixing the seeds with the feed of their horn'd Cattle & keeping the Cattle up till they have passed the seed—they then sprinkle this over their Land & plough it in, in the fall Season—in the Spring the seed will vegetate—as this process would be too late for this winter, I wou'd Recommend the mode I first proposed."

By June there is no lack of fruit to furnish the epergnes which stand on the dining tables in the Palace and the Wythe House. To my mind the Formal Dining Room in the Wythe House is the loveliest room in any of the exhibition buildings. The unusual yellow-gold shade of the curtains and chair seats, repeated in the painted back of the corner cupboard, can be picked up by the pineapples and lemons always available.

I am grateful for the addition and variation of cherries, plums, and red currants especially now that grapes are lacking. July brings the smooth-skinned nectarine cheek to cheek with the rough-skinned peach. There are figs and apricots, and, although they last not more than two days, both are particularly attractive in this room. To my thinking no fruit blends so well in the George Wythe dining room as the warm-colored apricot; it has a most perfect complexion.

Many flowers that bloom intermittently during these summer months continue in bloom throughout the autumn until frost, so that there is little hard and fast distinction between the months of their flowering. Butterfly weed, wild senna, Cupid's dart, turtlehead, feverfew, coreopsis, day lilies, black-eyed Susan, golden ragwort, the wild bergamot bee balm, loosestrife, sea lavender, and flowering spurge are excellent flowers that tie in well in any large arrangements. False dragonhead I use frequently and find valuable since it remains in bloom when other flowers flag behind.

Red Oswego bee balm, white daisies, sweet sultan, and the graceful white-flowered sprays of the sorrel tree bloom in July and are lovely together at this season. False dragonhead, a native plant that found great favor abroad, is a welcome addition now, as are hollyhocks, gladioli, sunflowers, nasturtiums, and the strawflowers. The sweet scabious and the tuberose come to their heyday at the latter end of summer.

I could never do anything with hollyhocks until I learned to treat them as I do the timid flowers; they reward me by remaining fresh for four days. I plunge the stalks immediately into boiling water for about ten minutes, then transfer them to a cold bath. Hollyhocks are striking additions to any bouquet and I like to place them in their light and dark pink shades against the russet-red damask in the Formal Dining Room at the Palace. They are extremely handsome also with cut-and-come-again sunflower and the rich green foliage of the sorrel tree.

Gladioli are gracious and stately additions to mixed bouquets, for they add both color and substance. They were known to the eighteenth century in a surprisingly wide range of color—pale yellow or sulphur, pale blue approaching white, pale flesh, deep red inclining to purple, and dusky yellow. The white variety was said to be fragrant and John Hill mentioned gladioli of a deep but beautiful purple at times so dark as to be almost black.

I make one arrangement in the two-handled Bristol delft vase that rarely fails to please. It consists of tuberoses, gladioli, China asters, African marigolds, calendulas, red and yellow prince's plume, artemisia, and goldenrod.

Nasturtiums I use with other flowers in the bricks, the bud vases, and the nine-fingered posy holder where they arrange happily and combine beautifully with the motif and color of the pattern of the containers. The double nasturtium is surprisingly no novelty. Robert Furber tells us that, like the tulip, it first demanded a great price and was valued as a rarity. Our own John Randolph tells us that nasturtiums were worthy of cultivation not only for their beautiful orange-colored flowers but also for their excellence in salads.

I use the tuberose frequently in midsummer arrangements. It is a good mixer and easy to work with. The eighteenth century came hardly by the double variety of this flower. It seems that a certain gentleman succeeded in raising tuberoses from seeds but "though he had such Plenty of the Roots, as to destroy some Hundreds," it was a long while before he could be persuaded to part with any of them.

The tuberose was a subject of much correspondence between John Custis and Peter Collinson. In 1736 Custis wrote that it was not correct for Collinson to suppose they were plentiful in America, adding "I never saw or heard of any being here before and wish I knew the management of them whether the[y] must be taken up every year and planted again or not." The following year, Collinson thinking it "a pitty you shou'd be without so fine a flower," sent Custis still more bulbs. At last, in 1739, Custis succeeded in flowering tuberoses to his liking.

It seems a trifle absurd, perhaps ungrateful, that with such a mass of material I should lament the fact that there were certain flowers unknown to the eighteenth century, and so unknown today in our buildings. Petunias, in their pastel shades and with their long-lasting quality, both in the garden and the house, are flowers I am always sorry I cannot use.

As July draws to a close the strident color note provided in June by the tawny day lily is taken up by the golds and oranges of French and African marigolds, sunflowers, nasturtiums, and zinnias, by the yellows and reds of goldenrod, cockscomb, prince's plume, and the long-continuing calendulas.

Yet, even at this time, it is possible to make a wonderfully cool and fresh arrangement by a lavish use of Queen Anne's lace and the long sprays of the sorrel tree. And, when August comes, flowers generally have softer colors, the rose and lavender of China asters, the delicate light blue of mist flower echoing in the latter end of the flowering year the first pale shades of spring. This is fortunate since there is a room in the Palace, the Parlor on the first floor, where orange is the one color I dare not use. Here the curtains are gold and the carpet has pink flowers. Because the needlework chair seats and table covers bring in many other soft tones, it is possible to use a variety of colors just so long as orange is not among them.

August gives us the China aster, "a glorious autumn flower" as Collinson called it. It is a gardener's adage that no flowers give more satisfaction in color and ease of arrangement. Blooming through August until the frost cuts them, their predominant shades of pale pink to rose and lavender to purple combine attractively with the amaranthine red and yellow prince's plume, with scarlet sage and blue lobelia, tuberose and flowering tobacco, marigold and goldenrod.

China asters turn the page. The link between late summer and early autumn, they are indeed as John Hill called them, "Articles of great Account."

IV. Golden Autumn Harvest

THE wind rustling the dry leaves of the corn stalks warns us that the flower year is drawing to its close. Yet the sunflower still turns to us; China asters, French and African marigolds and calendulas, summer phlox, and gladioli still stay for us. Sweet scabious and cockscomb, together with the blue and scarlet sage, lobelia, tuberose, mist flower, and false dragonhead, flowering tobacco and snapdragon, all these bloom bravely, even more brilliantly, throughout the last flowering weeks until frost withers them. It is surprising how long these late-blooming flowers will last. I remember one year when at the very end of September I was able to make a most generous bouquet of saltbush, Queen Anne's lace, Guernsey lily, calendula, zinnia, and the yellow prince's plume.

Everywhere in the fields and along the roadsides late goldenrod and native asters stand in massed array. Blooming in variety all through the fall, they are among the chief glories of the American autumn. These, like the phlox that John Hill described as "an elegant weed," were improved in England and given a place in the flower border. The asters were prized in the eighteenth century not only for the flower border but also as ideal decoration for halls and chimneys, flowering at a time when "few better Flowers appear."

Colonial Americans were surprised at the goldenrod's popularity in

England. On its native soil it was disdained like the peony which John Hill lamented was ignored on account of its familiarity. The *"yellow flower, called the 'Plain-Weed,'* which is the torment of the neighbouring farmer," wrote William Cobbett in his *American Gardener* of 1821, "has been, above all the plants in this world, chosen as the most conspicuous ornament of the front of the King of England's grandest palace, that of Hampton-Court, where, growing in a rich soil to the height of five or six feet, it, under the name of *'Golden Rod,'* nods over the whole length of the edge of a walk, three quarters of a mile long and, perhaps thirty feet wide, the most magnificent perhaps, in Europe." And he adds, "But, be not too hasty, American, in laughing at John Bull's king; for, I see, as a choice flower in *your* gardens, that still more pernicious European weed . . . the *Corn-Poppy.* . . . This is quite sufficient to show the power of *rarity* in affixing value on shrubs and flowers."

Surprising as it may be to us that goldenrod had, and still has, so large a place in English decoration, I myself use it constantly and in quantity, both fresh and dried. You will find it in Furber's August bouquet and throughout late summer into autumn you will find it constantly in mine. Graceful, delicate yet firm, long lasting, it is one of the most decorative of all our plants and one of the great stand-bys of autumn and winter decoration.

Gold, red, and green—these are still the predominant colors in flower arrangements at this season. Where gold is the main color motif in a room, as in the Upper Middle Room in the Palace, the plentiful yellow and orange tones are an easy and happy choice, the addition of red striking a good contrasting note. One of my favorite early autumn mixtures for this room is a combination of spiky crotalaria and the fruiting sprays of highbush cranberry, together with sunflowers, African marigolds, and goldenrod. At times, when there are not sufficient flowers for so large a group, I add some kind of foliage such as Tatarian honeysuckle or the ever-ready pine and bayberry.

As with every season, so even in the fall of the year there are newcomers. Two frail autumn flowers are sternbergia and the pale mauve colchicum, both known in different parts of the country as autumn crocus. The small yellow-petaled sternbergia, flowering among its leaves, makes good company in brick containers with the leafless colchicum. During the summer the leaves of the latter have disappeared, leaving the flowers to bloom unprotected. This characteristic earned for them the name "naked ladies," although Lady Skipwith is careful to say that the term was used only by the common people. Secretary Logan of Pennsylvania, however, had no qualms about being misunderstood when he asked a friend in England to send him "twenty-five naked ladies."

In Williamsburg we lay special claim to Lady Skipwith. A Scottish girl who married Sir Peyton Skipwith, she has left us in her "Garden Notes" slight but valuable information concerning the plants grown for interior decoration in the eighteenth century. Tradition has identified her as the ghost of the Wythe House. According to this legend, Lady Skipwith once returned in a rage from a ball having, like Cinderella, left one shoe behind. Now at midnight it is said the click of one high-heeled slipper, alternating with the soft tread of a stockinged foot, can be heard on the staircase. Unfortunately I have found no evidence to support the story or even the supposition that she lived at the

Orange in the oriental Lowestoft jardiniere repeats the autumn brilliance
of marigold, sunflower, and goldenrod

house, but that she was familiar with it I have no doubt. Sister-in-law of Colonel Henry Skipwith who lived in the Wythe House at the end of the century, she must often have visited him at Williamsburg.

And as we have a special claim to Lady Skipwith, so also have we a claim to sternbergia. Native of the southern shores of the Mediterranean, it has created its own legend in the New World. In early colonial days sternbergia flowered in the Palace Gardens. When the last royal governor fled, and both Palace and gardens fell on ruinous days, the gardeners of Williamsburg transplanted the bulbs to their own ground, just as gardeners today might do. It is from Williamsburg that sternbergia has found its way to other old gardens throughout Virginia. As the flower of the Williamsburg Garden Club, it is still held in special esteem here.

Above all, September and October are the months of harvest and of fruitfulness. Sometimes I think we fail to use fruit decoratively in our homes as often as we might well do. It is curious that fruit has always been the stepchild in decorative arrangement, for the porcelain makers, in modeling it purely for table decoration, have long realized its ornamental value.

Fruit of course has not the sentimental or romantic hold on our affections that flowers possess. Yet I feel that as colorful decoration it is superb; you have only to see how it glows with rich color in the dark days of the year and I think you will agree with me. Moreover, you may use fruit either with extreme simplicity or with superlative extravagance. You may have a handful of brightly colored crab apples in a pewter bowl or a silver epergne loaded with exotics encircled by a Della Robbia wreath.

Semitropical fruit from the West Indies was available in the eighteenth century. As we know from records, it was imported from Jamaica to New York where it was "almost as plentyful and cheap" as on its native soil. Today semitropical fruit is easily available to us from Florida and California. Virginia itself has ever been noted for its fruits. It was said that the land was so fertile you could sleep while the fruit was growing to its full perfection.

We are now able to have apples, lemons, limes, pears, and oranges throughout the year, and grapes are available from July through to March. Grapes with their lovely leaves and twisted stems have always been considered highly decorative and are a perennial motif among the great works of art both in pictures and sculpture. It is not surprising, therefore, that they almost always find a place in the Williamsburg fruit arrangements, and it is a happy coincidence that grapes are among our native fruits.

Lemons and green limes are invaluable. Much as foliage relieves the color mass of a flower arrangement, so lemons and limes enhance more highly colored fruit. A combination I use constantly is one of clustered green grapes, lemons, limes, and crab apples in a silver epergne.

Oranges are used only in the Wythe House for the reason that their color in no way blends with the Palace furnishings. Similarly, my use of the pineapple needs explanation. Available all the year round it is still, as in the eighteenth century, the king of fruits from a purely decorative point of view. It appears often in the Wythe House but rarely in the Palace. The epergne in the Wythe House is smaller than that in the Palace and one pineapple in a group of other fruits fits it perfectly. But the larger epergne in the Palace needs two pineapples to make a balanced arrangement and, if you have tried, you will I think agree that it is extremely difficult to arrange two pineapples satisfactorily in one dish. Perhaps the real answer lies in the fact that all kings, over whatever kingdoms they preside, like to lord it over their commoners alone; one king, one throne.

November's newcomer is the pomegranate. Invaluable as a flowering tree, it is no less so as an ornamental fruit. I have said that fruit holds little place in our affections but in my own case I should qualify this statement. For me the pomegranate is a notable exception.

The pomegranate is symbolic and has been used traditionally both in church and home decoration. I never handle the lovely fruit without remembering Peter Collinson's remark to John Bartram: "Don't," he pleaded, "use the Pomegranate inhospitably, a stranger that has come so far to pay his respect to thee. Don't turn him adrift in the wide world; but plant it against the south side of thy house, nail it close to the wall. In this manner it thrives wonderfully with us, and flowers beautifully and bears fruit this hot year."

Nor do I forget John Hill who, with his gift of excellent description and pleasing economy of words, remarked, "If left ungathered it will burst upon the Tree, and show its crimson Grains with vast Beauty."

Watermelons and muskmelons were much used formerly. These were kept a good part of the winter in dark cellars, the secret being first to break off the stem and then to burn the broken end with a red-hot iron, a treatment very similar to the one I give my timid flowers. I do not use melons in the epergnes because they are too large, but I have used them alone in the Palace Kitchen.

I cannot resist giving here John Hill's directions for gathering fruit and fresh flowers, words which I have echoed in our less pleasing modern language:

"Let any one examine the State of Plants in general, in Summer, and he will find it this; as the great Heat of the Day comes on, their Leaves begin to flag; and they droop more and more till the Cool of the Evening. The Reason is, the great Evaporation of their Juices by the Sun's Heat: they grow flaccid from toward Noon till near Sun-set: then the Heat is over, and the Dews refresh them: They continue recruiting and recovering during the whole Night, and they are firm and lively in the Morning.

"The Case is the same in Fruits, only it is not so easily perceived. At Noon they are exhausted and flattened, and they are heated to the Heart: all this renders them dead and unpleasing. They begin to recruit toward Evening, as the Leaves; and in the same Manner are in their full Perfection at early Morning. One Hour after Sun-rise is the Time for gathering them: this was the Secret of the successful Gardener, and this everyone should practise."

It may be asked why we do not decorate for Thanksgiving. The reason is that although festivals were kept to celebrate the gathered harvest and other occasions of public rejoicing, Thanksgiving as we know it was not, during the eighteenth century, universally observed as a fixed date.

I have also often been asked for the meaning and origin of the word "epergne." An epergne is a centerpiece for table decoration usually consisting of several grouped dishes for fruit, nuts, and condiments. The word comes from the French *épargne*, meaning a "sparing" or "saving," and so suggests that the epergne was intended to serve the

The epergne in the Governor's Palace

double purpose of allowing people to help themselves freely and of saving the constant passing and handing of small condiments.

The designs of the early and late eighteenth-century epergnes show marked differences, those of the latter period being more simple in design and therefore preferable for everyday use. This in turn suggests that the epergne may have been a forerunner of the dumbwaiter or Lazy Susan, made in wood, which is still in use today. Occasionally, when our silver epergnes are being cleaned, I use two gold baskets in the Palace and a silver basket in the Wythe House. Handsome as gold may be, however, I prefer silver for fruit.

It is fortunate that both fruit and flowers have, at this season, a more lasting quality. Autumn flowers have more stamina than the fugitive flowers of midsummer, and this allows me time to complete the harvest of dried materials.

I make many excursions from now until the end of November, cutting the late varieties of goldenrod, boneset, horseweed, and saltbush; the seed pods of the red horse chestnut, silver bell, milkweed, and evening primrose. I start cutting branches of leaves, beginning during the last two weeks of October with the yellow Norway maple, but I shall deal with this in detail under the winter months.

After the first frosts have dismissed the more tender flowers, I turn to chrysanthemums that alone have the power to survive. Only the little button chrysanthemums were known in the eighteenth century, in white, yellow, and red, but I use these sparingly and am careful to choose the present-day varieties nearest to those formerly known.

These chrysanthemums, mixed in with beech leaves, are colorful and welcome in a Chinese vase; yellow and bronze are the shades I use with beech. With fresh red strawflowers and red oak leaves I use white chrysanthemums. This combination looks particularly well in the much-used Bristol delft vase.

One shrub that flowers in October is the lovely tea shrub. The white flowers among their beautiful green leaves strike a fresh and cheerful note in any room.

Sorry I am that winter lies ahead. Yet, for the flower decorator, every season has its compensations and every harvester waits impatiently to see his winter store.

V. Winter's Pleasant Ornaments

I ALWAYS welcome the first cold November day when I go to the plant drying room. I pull open the door and look about much as a farmer surveys his stored grain in the barn. I unpack the leaves to see if they have pressed properly; I take down the bunches of dried materials to discover if they were gathered at just the right moment to assure their handling well. It is time to make flower arrangements that will last three months instead of three short days.

In preparing dried plant material for winter decoration a proper drying room is an absolute necessity. It is every bit as important to the winter decorator as tools are to the gardener. The drying room should be a shade warmer than outside and never in the least bit damp—it must be bone dry. The room should also be as dark as possible since the plants retain their original colors to a far greater extent if allowed to mature in darkness. The importance of a dry, dark room was known to Philip Miller who wrote of the globe amaranth, "These Flowers, if gathered before they decay on the Plant, and kept in a dry Place, will remain in Beauty for some Years, especially if they are not too much expos'd to the Air." When mixed with other varieties, he continued, they will "make a curious Variety of dry Flowers for Basons to adorn Rooms in the Winter Season, when few other Kinds are to be had."

In Williamsburg the upper story of the Palace Kitchen serves as my

49

drying room. Here wires are strung from wall to wall and each bunch of flowers is tied and hung up as soon as gathered. The windows are small and are blacked out either with cloth or with paper. Once the flowers are completely dried and their colors "set," they will not fade even if, in their final arrangement, they are placed in a sunny window.

Harvesting materials at the proper time is as important as the drying room. I can only give the approximate time for gathering because choosing the right moment is a matter of experience, and the seasons vary. But generally plants should be gathered at their prime, in the first flush of their bloom just as they reach their full color. The process of flowering seems to continue after they are bunched and hung up. You will see how the blooms fluff up and are yet held so compactly to the flower structure that they do not shatter when later you handle them for their final arrangement.

Looking back over the summer and autumn months I realize how wide has been my choice of material; as wide as anyone would wish. Not only have I used a variety of garden plants, but along the streams, by roadsides, and in the fields and woods I have gathered like a squirrel for my winter store. Wild flowers, ferns, and grasses; seed pods, ears of wheat, and corn tassels; common weeds and autumn leaves, they have all been there for the gathering.

I was once amused when a flower decorator visiting Williamsburg reported she had heard from a friend that I had the assistance of twelve college students to scour the country for a fifty-mile radius, and so had no difficulty in obtaining all the plant material needed. Actually I have the help of a driver and one assistant once or twice a week for a couple

First glimpse of winter's pleasant ornaments

Harvest from field and garden

A winter bouquet

From sand-filled container shown on the opposite page
to the finished dried arrangement above

A Christmas wreath inspired by Della Robbia medallions

William Williams helping to gather flowers in the cutting garden

The portrait of Charles II in the Ballroom of the Governor's Palace

of hours at a time. A station wagon is set aside for my use on these occasions, and into it we must load all that we have harvested. I marveled how rumor had blown like the autumn wind, scattering and gathering afresh as it went.

During the summer months I have gathered, bunched, and hung upside down to await the November day when I should use them, everlastings, honesty, and the purple-cupped sea lavender that Lady Skipwith dried for her mantelpiece; bittersweet, blazing star, and hydrangea in various stages of color; scarlet sage and purple Yorktown onions.

All these greet me when I open the drying-room door. As I handle the strawflowers I remember the days of their gathering, days when the earth itself was burnt to a pale straw color of dust and dryness under high blue skies. Indeed their very name is reminiscent of harvest. Especially loved and frequently used in older days, they came both white and purple, single and double, and the gardeners who grew them for the winter market stained them deep red and blue. So London bought them, white, purple, blue, and red.

The globe amaranth was also treasured in the eighteenth century for indoor decoration. Peter Collinson writing to John Custis in Williamsburg said, "I am much Delighted to heare you have your amaranthoides It is a Real & I may say perpetual Beauty. If the flowers are gather'd in perfection and hung up with their Heads Downwards in a Dry shady Room, they will keep thear Colours for years and will make a pleasant Ornament to Adorn the Windows of your parlor or study all the Winter. I Dry great Quantities for that purpose and putt them in flower potts & China basons & they make a fine show all the Winter."

I look too at the ferns that I gathered in the woods in June: cinnamon fern and royal fern, pressed between layers of paper. I find these invaluable because they retain their green color, and I can use them to add a touch of lightness to the dried bouquets much as a cook will use herbs for seasoning. There is joe-pye weed gathered in August; bone-set, horseweed, and saltbush cut in October; cattails that have been waiting since June. Dock is there, cut at various stages from June, when the delicate tan color held many rosy tints, on through August, when the seeding stalk was brown as rust.

Goldenrod too was gathered in variety from July up until frost—the wreath, the silver, and the wrinkled goldenrod, Canada, plume, and fragrant. It is important that goldenrod should be cut at just the right time. If it is gathered too soon it will give only a thin lacy effect, remaining without further development just as it was when cut; if harvested in its prime, however, you will find when you come to arrange it that the dried heads will not shatter as you might expect of a flower that becomes so brittle when dried.

And pearly everlastings. These I treasure for their association as well as for their use. I love their amaranthine quality, their constancy in standing in the open fields, unwithering in bloom. As I gather them I think of the first women colonists who, as Peter Kalm tells us, found them growing in great quantities, and gathered them for winter decoration, calling them life everlasting for their changelessness, fresh or dried.

Silken corn tassels, golden wheat, pale oats, and bearded barley greet me as do the grasses, an army of them: cloud grass, marrom grass, broom-sedge grass, plume, spike and fox-tail grass, and many others.

Last, but not least, the leaves. Of all the dried materials these are the most important. I gather the branches when the leaves are at the height of their color yet still full of sap. This again is something to be learned by experience, for you will find that if cut too late the leaves, when you come to unpack and lift the branches, will flutter to the floor. Nevertheless there are some, such as beech, that may be gathered still green, or others, such as dogwood, that may be gathered when partly green and partly red. Both are effective in green arrangements or for variety of contrasting effects.

Many trips to the woods are needed for a wide choice of leaf color, and every individual tree has its own proper season for turning. Here in Williamsburg the yellow Norway maples are among the first to be gathered, usually during the last two weeks of October. These are followed by the sugar maple with its beautiful orange-red shades and the red maple with its brilliant red tones.

Beech leaves may be collected here for several weeks and have proved themselves best for yellow effects in arrangements. Dogwood may be gathered for about two weeks either when the leaves are still partly green or when they have turned to their full autumn red. Sassafras and sorrel tree can be used, but in Williamsburg we have found that scarlet oak, the red and yellow maples, dogwood, hickory, and beech serve us better.

In gathering these leaves care must be taken to select only those branches that are perfectly flat. They should be put immediately into a vessel of water to keep them from wilting and brought thus into the drying room. There they are placed on the floor for trimming and, this done, placed between papers where they should lie perfectly flat, with no two leaves overlapping. As many layers of leaves may be piled one on the other as required, but it is essential that paper separate each layer. Finally a flat frame made of heavy wood is placed on top, and additional weights added. In about three weeks the leaves will be ready to use but unless they are perfectly dry they will curl.

When I come to arrange the dried material, I take the containers I have chosen to the drying room for, even though the material has been properly treated, making a dried arrangement is rather a messy affair.

Sand, as in the eighteenth century, is still the ideal material with which to hold the dried leaves and flowers in the containers. Among the illustrations is a set of four which shows how I go about making the very full arrangements destined for the large rooms. Real buxom bouquets. First I select the branches of leaves and with them trace the outline. Gradually I fill in with the other materials in the required colors, working from the top down to the base. There I mass the more solid flowers, the strawflowers, prince's plumes, and yarrow, placing the lighter pearly everlastings and sea lavender above. White I use a great deal both as a filler and to lighten the whole arrangement. For this purpose quantities of boneset, pearly everlasting, and saltbush are effective.

Generally speaking I use white as my chief filler in making the red-toned arrangements, and goldenrod for the predominantly yellow ones. You will be surprised to discover how much material it takes to make even one full arrangement, and will understand why I gather such large amounts of goldenrod and white materials.

The dried bouquets are arranged in the same printy manner as the fresh flowers. A combination of yellow beech leaves and green ferns, yellow strawflowers and red horse-chestnut pods, yellow cockscomb and bittersweet look well together in a pewter vase and are very much at home in a man's room. A jardiniere of white Wedgwood lends crisp contrast to the reds, yellows, and greens of red and yellow maple leaves, green dogwood, yellow yarrow, artemisia, red prince's plume, cockscomb, and blazing star. Together these give a happy balance to both leaves and flowers.

I find that a predominantly red arrangement looks well in the Bristol delft vase—red prince's plume, red maple leaves, saltbush, honesty, green ferns, blazing star, and white and red strawflowers; these all make a brilliant and glowing arrangement. For contrast I like pressed green ferns, yellow and green beech leaves, Yorktown onions, white pearly everlasting, honesty, green hydrangea, various brown and tan grasses, yellow, orange, and brown strawflowers, lavender joe-pye weed, and white boneset in a large glass goblet.

It can readily be understood that although I am somewhat restricted in both the material and style of arrangement, yet variety is infinite. As I arrange my dried bouquets I get an added pleasure from remembering how long they will last. So, with the dried arrangements all set in their respective places, I turn with a little leisure and welcome respite to planning the Christmas decorations.

Of all decorations those at Christmas show a greater continuity of tradition and style than those of any other season. Houses and churches have been decked with evergreens from the early days of history, for the custom is of pagan origin.

From the earliest times "bringing home Christmas" has meant gathering evergreens from the woods. Yew and holly, gathered for their red berries as much as for the sake of their greenery, have ever been the mainstays of Christmas garlanding. But "whatsoever the year afforded to be green" has also found a place, so I use box, pine, and fir; bayberry, ivy, and rosemary; cherry laurel, aucuba leaves, and the storied mistletoe.

Additionally I use pine cones, honesty, wheat, and other dried materials such as strawflowers and red prince's plume, which lend an added eighteenth-century touch. Fruit and nuts in variety—all are grist to my mill.

Christmas calls for special arrangements on each dining-room table and these are deliberately modeled on the old fruit prints or the work of the fifteenth-century Italian sculptor Luca Della Robbia. Della Robbia's brilliantly colored garlands of flowers and fruits—notably apples, lemons, oranges, fir cones, and leaves—were not only exceptionally beautiful but so accurate in detail that it is said no botanist could ever quarrel with them. One of the most successful adaptations I ever made of his garlands was a large Christmas wreath of magnolia leaves, red cedar, crisp scarlet oak leaves, pomegranates, and green grapes. Eight large groupings of fruit, accented by magnolia leaves, surrounded the epergne on the lovely mahogany table in the Formal Dining Room of the Palace. The rest of the wreath was filled in with soft red cedar and scarlet oak leaves.

Since these Christmas decorations are kept in the buildings for two weeks, there is an advantage in this type of arrangement for I am able to keep the materials fresh by replacing the fruit and greens when necessary. In addition to the special arrangements for the dining-room tables and the mantels and window seats, every window has its wreath and candle so that for two weeks the Williamsburg nights are bright.

For the exterior Christmas decorations I buy a great quantity of garlands of mountain laurel or of white pine. These I use lavishly on balconies, on wrought-iron gates, and around doorways. This is quite an undertaking and requires the services of two experienced carpenters from the Maintenance Department.

Christmas decorations are kept in the buildings from Christmas Eve until January 6, the Feast of the Epiphany. On that day we do as Herrick bid us:

> Down with the rosemary and so
> Down with the baies and misletoe;
> Down with the holly, ivie, all
> Wherewith you drest the Christmas hall.

Throughout January and February the dried flower arrangements, together with the fruit and greens, are the main decoration. As addition and variation I use certain potted plants which take their place happily with the evergreens. Of these, lantana, as Lady Skipwith noted, is seldom without flowers and cyclamen continues in bloom until late spring.

Thus helped through the flowers' winter sleep, it is not long until spring welcomes us again with hyacinth and daffodils that come to deck another "dancing Easter-day."

VI. Familiar Friends

⁂

THE story of gardening is but a branch of the tree of history. There is nothing, I think, that brings us into such close intimacy with the past as flowers; nothing that bridges the years in quite the same way. Words change their meaning and like music can be interpreted in many ways: the colors of a picture fade, but plants have much the same significance in every age the world over.

Pick a bud of sweet shrub and crush it in your hand or fold it in your handkerchief. The fragrance is as fresh as it was the day John Bartram first found the flower more than two hundred years ago.

To us in Virginia, Jefferson's *Garden Book* means much more than a record of the flowers he grew. It gives us a direct link with the past to know that one year his pinks and hollyhocks bloomed on the tenth of June; that on the eighteenth argemone put out one flower.

One flower. I sometimes think this the most significant note in all my journeys through the old records. It is typical of the period that Jefferson, in all his everyday busyness, should not only find time to make exact notes, but should think it worth while to observe and record the detail of a single bloom.

It is typical because the eighteenth century, a time of political excitement, of national expansion, and scientific exploration—and therefore of transition—was yet, perhaps more than any other age, stamped with a distinct identity. Good living was its hallmark. It was an age of curiosity and craftsmanship, of design and detail. And if it was an age of elegance and ease it was, equally, one of industry and achievement.

This transition and expansion is reflected in the eighteenth-century horticultural world. In the long history of gardening there never was so great an age, so amazing a variety of garden developments.

From east to west some of the greatest plant shipments in garden history were carried through. In Russia, Peter the Great ordered forty thousand forest trees to be dug, carried, and replanted for the landscaping of the Peterhof. In France, Le Notre brought three thousand young orange trees from Italy and transplanted, on another occasion, twenty five thousand trees from other parts of France to furnish the great garden at Versailles. All over Europe, in France, Sweden, Switzerland, Austria, and Holland, men were avidly interested in gardening.

With the search for new lands came the discovery of a wealth of fresh plant material. The New World began to unfold its treasures. With the migration of people came a migration of plants. During the first half of the eighteenth century about three hundred and twenty new flowers and shrubs were introduced into England from North America. At the same time the English colonists in America, eagerly cultivating the newly discovered native plants, lost no opportunity to introduce and establish the old familiar flowers of their homeland, especially those considered to be essential in a gentleman's garden. A dazzle of color was beginning to supersede the "green thought in a green shade."

This was the period when the first botanical gardens were established —John Bartram's by the Schuylkill River near Philadelphia and the Chelsea Physic Garden and Kew Gardens in England. New tools were invented, old ones improved. Above all, garden designs were radically changing. Formalism was on the wane.

In England the revolt against formalism swept away the trim patterned gardens in the Dutch and French style. The long vistas of the naturalistic landscape garden which replaced them were, in their expansiveness and broadened horizons, a reflection of the mood of the period.

The new landscape style was firmly established in England by the middle of the century but came more slowly to America. Here the formal garden lingered for a long time. For this reason the green gardens of Williamsburg, like those of most of the estates throughout Virginia, are laid out in the formal style.

Similarly the new ideas filtering throughout Europe from far-away China were, to a great extent, spent before reaching England, and were seen there only in Oriental garden features, in wallpaper and porcelains, and in the furniture designs of Chippendale. But this Chinese influence eventually reached even Williamsburg, which explains why you will see evidence of it today in the flower containers and the wallpapers that are the background to some of my arrangements. Still later, after the turn of the century, England and America also introduced into their gardens great quantities of plant material from China.

The eighteenth century was an age of amateur as well as professional gardeners. Botany was not only an integral part of scientific investigation but, among the educated, was studied and pursued as a fashionable hobby. It was a hobby shared by merchants, sea captains, noblemen, politicians, doctors, bishops, lawyers, ambassadors, and governors. Each made some contribution to this common interest.

Behind the plantsmen in the field was a whole army of men recording by correspondence, by books and journals, the story of eighteenth-century discoveries. Men not only sought new plants; they also strove to classify and study their improvement.

In America John Bartram was the first, in 1739, to experiment in hybridization. The following year Thomas Fairchild, in England, though he blushed thinking it unnatural and immoral, obtained the first known hybrid pink from a crossing between a carnation and a sweet William. In Sweden, Linnaeus was working out the principles for defining the genera and species of plants, and we have ever since universally used the system of binomial nomenclature which he established.

In my research on the authentic use of plants in flower decoration, I have come to think of the great plantsmen as my familiar friends. I have found that in the long procession of famous names in eighteenth-century garden history all but a few were directly or indirectly associated with Williamsburg. Many famous travelers and botanists passed through the capital; others throughout colonial America and Europe were known to Williamsburg horticulturists by correspondence and the exchange of plant material.

During the heyday of Williamsburg its people, from governors to the humblest of property owners, were garden-minded. John Custis, a leading citizen and a member of the Governor's Council, has a special claim on our interest as the kingpin of Williamsburg's amateur gardeners and the possessor of the finest collection of lilacs in America at that time. He lived on what are now the grounds of Eastern State Hospital. Although his house and garden have disappeared, one ancient yew tree, which I like to think may have been planted by his own hand, still stands near the old brick Custis Kitchen. Of no particular fame in garden history, Custis was yet known personally to many botanists and exchanged plants and corresponded with many more. He was, moreover, related to famous men, for he was brother-in-law to William Byrd II and father-in-law to Martha Dandridge who, after the death of her first husband Daniel Parke Custis, became Mrs. George Washington.

William Byrd II, a member of the Council of Virginia, owned property on the Duke of Gloucester Street. A wealthy and cultured eighteenth-century Virginian, his estate at near-by Westover on the James was notable for its gardens.

George Washington, for many years before his courtship of Martha Dandridge, visited Williamsburg frequently as a burgess and military leader. On his marriage he acquired control of her property in and around Williamsburg, overseeing it with a keen and constant interest. His garden at Mount Vernon, and the meticulous record of his plantings there, are monuments to his skill and interest in gardening.

Several eighteenth-century governors of Virginia, including Alexander Spotswood, Francis Fauquier, and Thomas Jefferson, were keen gardeners. Williamsburg knew Jefferson intimately, not only in the days of his governorship, when he lived for some months at the Palace, but also in his youth. He attended the College of William and Mary and studied law under George Wythe in the house on Palace Green which now bears Wythe's name. Remembered by horticulturists for his garden at Monticello and his *Garden Book*, which today is a valuable addition to early American garden history, Jefferson also exchanged

Autumn gold captured in a Chinese posy holder

much plant material with European horticulturists; he sent American species to the Jardin des Plantes in Paris, and while in France and England, shipped many new varieties back to his own garden at Monticello.

John Custis was near neighbor to Sir John Randolph, a prominent attorney of Williamsburg. The Custis pleasure garden was but a stone's throw from Randolph's kitchen garden, both situated south of Francis Street. Sir John Randolph's son John wrote *A Treatise on Gardening*, the first American work on kitchen gardening to give instructions for raising vegetables in the climate of Virginia, very different from that of England on which all previous instructions had been based.

Other garden associates in Williamsburg included Dr. John M. Galt, surgeon and doctor to the mental hospital, who is remembered for his introduction of Scotch broom, and Joseph Prentis, who left a meticulous record of the vegetables he raised in his Williamsburg garden.

John Clayton, for whom the lovely little flower spring beauty, *Claytonia virginica*, is named, came to America at the age of about twenty when his father was appointed Recorder of Williamsburg. As Clerk of Gloucester County he subsequently lived at Windsor, in that part of Gloucester now Mathews County, where he devoted his leisure to the study of Virginia plants. His collection was later sent to the Dutch botanist Gronovius, who, working with Linnaeus, described and classified the plants, publishing a list of them as *Flora Virginica*, a book which has since proved of great value in the study of the plant life of the colony. The work has additional interest and unique value in that, whereas the long and complicated nomenclature in general use at that time was employed in the first edition, the new nomenclature of Linnaeus appeared in the second.

Famous botanists from across the water who came to Williamsburg include Mark Catesby, John Banister, and John Mitchell. Of these Catesby is best known. An English naturalist, he first became interested in Virginia through the marriage of his sister to Dr. William Cocke of Williamsburg, Secretary of the Colony. We are proud at Colonial Williamsburg to possess a copy of his *History of Carolina, Florida, and the Bahama Islands,* the most sumptuous book of its kind to be published in the eighteenth century.

John Banister was a missionary and botanist sent to Virginia by Henry Compton, Bishop of London and close friend of James Blair, first President of the College of William and Mary. Banister's *A Catalogue of Plants in Virginia* was published in England by John Ray, and like John Clayton's plant list, is still of much value and interest.

John Mitchell, for many years a physician of Urbanna, was one of Virginia's most distinguished botanists. We remember him by the partridgeberry which Linnaeus named *Mitchella repens* in his honor.

But unquestionably the most famous plantsman to pass through Williamsburg was John Bartram of Philadelphia, whom Linnaeus called the greatest natural botanist in the world. Traveling thousands of miles through unchartered, unsettled eastern America, sometimes alone and sometimes with his son William, Bartram collected plants for dried specimens and seeds for American and European gardens. Among his discoveries are the silver bell, the sweet shrub, the Catawba rhododendron, and the rare and beautiful Franklinia which was named after Benjamin Franklin, his lifelong friend and supporter.

On his trip to Virginia in 1738 Bartram carried introductions to John Custis, William Byrd II, and Isham Randolph. In a letter to Peter Collinson in England, he wrote, "I have performed my journey through Maryland and Virginia, as far as Williamsburgh, so up James River to the mountains, so over and between the mountains, in many very crooked turnings and windings, in which according to the nearest computation I can make, betwixt my setting out and returning home, I travelled 1100 miles in five weeks' time; having rested but one day in all that time, and that was at Williamsburgh."

And as John Custis was the kingpin of the Williamsburg garden world, so John Bartram was the kingpin of the American horticultural world. He was to find in Peter Collinson, a city-bred woolen merchant of London, his English counterpart.

Peter Collinson devoted all his leisure to an immense correspondence and exchange of plants with botanists all over the world. Accepting and expecting no remuneration, he worked as a self-imposed duty; he explained that "As the nobility and gentry have for some years past introduced a great variety of North American trees, shrubs and flowers into their plantations, the present as well as the next generation may be pleased to know at what time and by whom such abundance of the vegetable production of our colonies were naturalised to our climate."

Both Bartram and Collinson were in touch with almost every botanist of note of their day. Their correspondence with each other covers a period of thirty-eight years (Collinson additionally acting as Bartram's agent with his English patrons), and John Custis corresponded with Collinson between 1734-1746.

Though it is beyond the scope of this brief historical sketch to name all of the many gardeners who either through John Custis, John Bartram, or Peter Collinson were interested in Williamsburg, mention must be made of a few: the Swedish explorer Peter Kalm, for instance, after whom Linnaeus named the mountain laurel, *Kalmia latifolia*; Alexander Garden, physician and naturalist of Charleston, South Carolina, whom we remember by the gardenia; Mrs. Martha Logan, also of Charleston, who at the age of seventy wrote the *Gardener's Kalender*.

There was also Philip Miller, curator of the Chelsea Physic Garden in London. He was known to Williamsburg through correspondence, and his book, *The Gardeners Dictionary*, found a place in the libraries of Lord Botetourt, Thomas Lord Fairfax, Daniel Parke Custis, and John Randolph. As Mark Catesby's *History* was the most sumptuous plant book of the century, so Miller's *Gardeners Dictionary* was the most universally used and valued garden book of the period, both in America and England.

The enormous accomplishment of the eighteenth-century horticulturists is almost unbelievable when we remember the conditions under which they worked. In our age of swift communication, when newspapers carry daily columns on gardening, when garden clubs are a part of most communities, and when gigantic flower shows annually draw thousands of visitors from every part of the land, we forget that in the eighteenth century travel was not only slow, but dangerous. We forget that letters between America and England, written slowly and meticulously by quill, took three months to reach their destination instead of the present three days by air; that plants frequently died in transit. The disappointments of the early botanists might well have discouraged less determined men.

Peering across the years I can see a man bending close to the candle's flame, reading a letter. I see him, with trembling fingers, untie a little silk bag and spread the seeds out in the palm of his hand before laying them on the table. What they are, I do not know, I cannot see, but they might well be the seeds of Virgin Stock that Mrs. Logan from far-off Charleston sent in just such a little silk bag to John Bartram. His pleasure, though perhaps more intense, is not unlike our own when we scan the year's catalogues to see what we can try that is new.

I like to remember these early "brothers of the spade." I like to know that in Williamsburg we keep their memory as we keep their gardens, ever green.

Some Eighteenth-Century Plantsmen

Brief notes on some of the chief men in the
eighteenth-century horticultural world who, directly or indirectly,
were connected with Williamsburg.

John BANISTER, 1650-1692

English naturalist and missionary, Banister was sent over by Henry Compton, Bishop of London, to the West Indies and Virginia, where he lived for many years in Charles City County. John Ray, to whom he sent a list of Virginia plants, published in England Banister's *Catalogue of Plants Observed in Virginia.*

John BARTRAM, 1699-1777

Called by Linnaeus "the greatest natural botanist in the world," John Bartram was one of the most illustrious of the early American botanists. He traveled throughout eastern North America collecting seeds and plants, and by their distribution to the eminent horticulturists of his day, he became the chief link in the exchange of plant material between Europe and America. It is estimated that he introduced into England and the Continent between 150 and 200 plants.

Bartram was the first in America to experiment in hybridizing and to use the Linnaean system of plant classification; he also established in

1728 the first botanical garden in America at Kingsessing on the Schuylkill River near Philadelphia.

William BARTRAM, 1739-1823

The son of John Bartram, William was a prominent botanist in his own right and an able artist. He continued the travels he had begun with his father, and his book *Travels through North and South Carolina, Georgia, East and West Florida* was widely read and inspired Wordsworth, Coleridge, and other writers. As an artist he was commissioned by the Duchess of Portland in England to paint land and water shells.

William BYRD II, 1674-1744

Virginia born, William Byrd was educated in England. Returning to Virginia in 1692 as heir to a large estate, he came to typify the grace, charm, and culture of the Virginians of the eighteenth century. A close friend of many prominent men in America and England, Byrd was a Fellow of the Royal Society in England, a member of the Council of Virginia, and a fine horticulturist. His estate at Westover was famous, and many references to plants are found in his *Secret Diary* and *Natural History of Virginia*.

Mark CATESBY, c.1679-1749

Born at Sudbury, Suffolk, England, Catesby's interest in Virginia began through the marriage of his sister, Elizabeth, to Dr. William Cocke of Williamsburg, Secretary of the Colony. Catesby stayed in Virginia from 1712 to 1719 when he returned to England. In 1722 he came back to America and spent four more years in travel. The result

John Custis of Williamsburg from the original portrait in the
Lee Chapel at Washington and Lee University

Original Furber prints on the staircase wall of the George Wythe House

of the second expedition appeared in *The Natural History of Carolina, Florida, and the Bahama Islands*, published in two volumes in 1731, 1743.

John CLAYTON, c.1685-1773

Born at Fulham, Kent, England, Clayton came to Virginia when he was about twenty with his father who in 1714 was appointed Attorney-General at Williamsburg. In 1722 John Clayton was named Clerk of Gloucester County, a post he held until his death. Thomas Jefferson wrote of him "This accurate observer was a native and resident of this state, passed a long life in exploring and describing its plants, and is supposed to have enlarged the botanical catalogue as much as almost any man who has lived." The Dutch botanist Gronovius, in collaboration with Linnaeus, classified botanically a list of native plants sent him by Clayton, and published it as *Flora Virginica*.

Peter COLLINSON, 1694-1768

Peter Collinson, Quaker woolen merchant of London, was probably the greatest horticultural correspondent of all time. He corresponded with John Bartram for thirty-eight years and also with all Bartram's English patrons. He is believed to have introduced more than forty American plants into English gardens, in addition to collecting and importing seeds of new and unusual plants from all over the world. By the middle of the century his garden at Mill Hill had become a famous plant center. A member of the Royal Society of England and a great benefactor to many men, Collinson substantially added to Sir Hans Sloane's manuscript collection which later became the nucleus of the natural history section of the British Museum.

Henry COMPTON, 1632-1713

It was through the influence of Compton, Bishop of London, that the charter of the College of William and Mary was secured in 1693. As its adviser, patron, and supporter in England, Compton was made first Chancellor of the college. He gathered exotic plants from all parts of the world in his famous garden at Fulham in Kent, and it was he who sent John Banister to the West Indies and Virginia as botanist and missionary.

John CUSTIS, 1678-1749

Custis, known as John Custis of Williamsburg, was a member of the Council of Virginia for twenty-two years. A correspondent of Peter Collinson from 1734 to 1746, he was an enthusiastic horticulturist. In his garden south of Francis Street he had the best collection of lilacs in North America, and Bartram reported that only John Clayton's garden was better furnished. John Custis was the brother-in-law of William Byrd II of Westover and his daughter-in-law, Martha Dandridge, married George Washington after the death of her first husband, Daniel Parke Custis.

Thomas FAIRCHILD, 1667-1729

Established about 1693 as a nurseryman and florist of Hoxton, England, Fairchild was the first in that country to prove by experiment the existence of sex in plants, and the first to produce scientifically an artificial hybrid pink by crossing a carnation and a sweet William. Of this, Collinson wrote to Bartram: "It has the leaves of the first, and its flowers double like a Carnation—the size of a Pink,—but in clusters like the Sweet William. It is named a *Mule*,—per analogy to the mule produced from the Horse and Ass."

Francis FAUQUIER, 1704-1768

Son of a director of the Bank of England, Fauquier served as Lieutenant-Governor of Virginia from 1758 to 1768, during which time he resided in the Governor's Palace. A Fellow of the Royal Society of London, he was deeply interested in horticulture, a good musician, and an ardent gambler. He is buried in Bruton Parish Church in Williamsburg.

John FOTHERGILL, 1712-1780

Quaker and London physician, Fothergill became on Collinson's death Bartram's chief English correspondent. Like Collinson he introduced into England many new plants from North America, and his garden, at Upton, near Stratford, once rivaled Kew Gardens.

Robert FURBER, — - —

Nurseryman of Kensington, near London, Furber published in 1730 a series of twelve large colored flower plates entitled *Twelve Months of Flowers*, and a similar series on fruits. Each plate purports to show all the flowers or fruits which bloom or ripen for that month. A second edition of the flower catalogue, published in 1732, included a text and a new title, *The Flower-Garden Display'd*.

Alexander GARDEN, c.1730-1791

It was Alexander Garden, physician and naturalist of Charleston, South Carolina, for whom Linnaeus, at the request of John Ellis, named the gardenia. Garden started a nursery on his estate at Oranto, near Charleston, and was the author of *Flora Carolina*. He also corresponded with many of the chief botanists of his time.

Jan Frederick GRONOVIUS, 1690-1760

It was Gronovius, an eminent Dutch botanist of Leyden, who persuaded Linnaeus to publish his *Systema Naturae*. He was also responsible, in collaboration with Linnaeus, for the publication of Clayton's *Flora Virginica*.

John HILL, c.1716-1775

Chiefly remembered today for *The British Herbal*, 1756, and his often quoted *Eden*, 1757, Hill also wrote a monumental work in twenty-six volumes called *The Vegetable System* and was a prolific author of novels and plays as well. A practicing apothecary, he made considerable sums from the preparation of vegetable medicines.

Thomas JEFFERSON, 1743-1826

Jefferson was educated at the College of William and Mary at Williamsburg and studied law under George Wythe. He was twice Governor of Virginia. A great amateur horticulturist, Jefferson himself planned the garden at Monticello. His *Garden Book*, begun in 1766, is still of interest today.

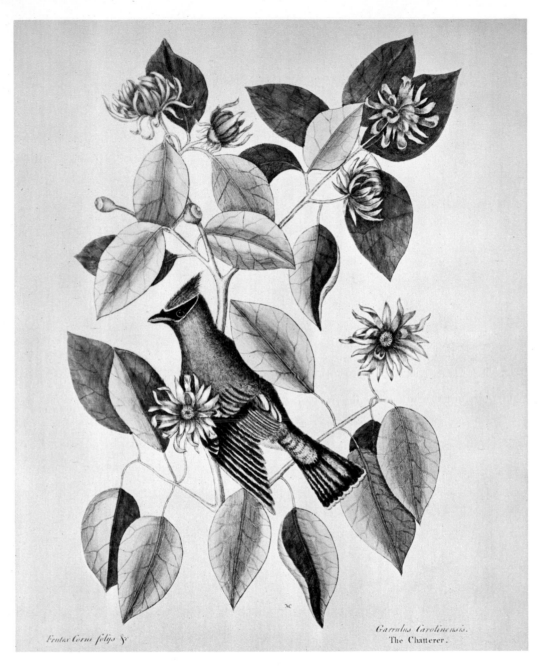

Frutex Corni folijs &c

Garrulus Carolinensis.
The Chatterer.

The sweet shrub from Mark Catesby's *Natural History*

Catesby's engraving of the mountain laurel, named *Kalmia latifolia*
in honor of Peter Kalm

Peter KALM, 1715-1779

Peter Kalm, a Swedish botanist, recorded his journey through the colonies in *Travels into North America*. Kalm was a favorite pupil of Linnaeus who named the mountain laurel, *Kalmia latifolia*, for him.

John LAWSON, ——-1711

Possessed by a wanderlust, the Englishman John Lawson sailed to New York and from there, being told that "Carolina was the best country" to fit his mood for further travel, he set off for Charleston. Without guides, but accompanied by six other Englishmen, he explored the Carolina wilderness, followed Indian trails, and finally took the trading path that ran through Georgia to Bermuda Hundred on the south side of the James River in Virginia. He recorded his travels in *A New Voyage to Carolina*. Later appointed Survey-General of North Carolina, he was murdered by the Indians on a subsequent plant expedition.

Henry LAURENS, 1724-1792

A leading citizen of Charleston, South Carolina, Laurens introduced olives, capers, limes, ginger, the alpine strawberry, red raspberries, and blue grapes to America. He also imported apples, pears, plums, and wine grapes from France.

Carolus LINNAEUS, 1707-1778

Linnaeus, a Swede, is known as the Father of Botany. As the author of a system of binomial nomenclature, he was the first to lay down the principles for defining the genera and species of plants.

James LOGAN, 1674-1751

As President and senior member of the Provincial Council of Pennsylvania, Logan was the chief executive of the Province during the Governor's absence from 1736 to 1738, and hence is often referred to as Governor Logan. A keen student of horticulture, he encouraged John Bartram and sent Indians up the Susquehanna River to procure the great American laurel, *Rhododendron maximum*. His gardens at Stenton, four miles north of Philadelphia, became famous, and were notable for a fine avenue of hemlocks. Logan's essay *Experimenta et Meletemata de Plantarum generatione*, published at Leyden in 1739, describes his observations on pollen grains and illustrates Linnaeus's theory of the sexes of plants.

Martha Daniel LOGAN, 1702-1779

Described as "a great florist and uncommonly fond of a garden," Mrs. Logan was a correspondent of John Bartram and other botanists. At the age of seventy she wrote *The Gardener's Kalendar*. This volume, published after her death, continued to influence gardening until about 1808.

John MITCHELL, ——-1768

After many years as a physician in Urbanna, Virginia, Mitchell returned to his native London toward the end of his life. One of Virginia's most distinguished botanists, he was among the first to grasp and apply the Linnaean classification of plants. Naturalist and cartographer, he was the author of many works, including *Nova Plantarum*

Genera which contained the first mention of the penstemon or beard tongue. Mitchell was a friend of Bartram and Peter Kalm, and corresponded with many other botanists. He is remembered in the partridgeberry, *Mitchella repens*.

Bernard MacMAHON, c.1775-1816

MacMahon, a Philadelphia nurseryman and seed collector, was also the author of various works including *The American Gardener's Calendar*, 1806.

Philip MILLER, 1691-1771

Curator of the Chelsea Physic Garden, London, Miller edited *The Gardeners Dictionary*, the most important garden book of his time. It was translated into Dutch, French, and German, and was the standard authority for at least a century both in America and England.

Isham RANDOLPH, 1685-1742

A keen horticulturist, Isham Randolph of Dungeness, Goochland County, was burgess for Goochland from 1736 until 1740. He was the grandfather of Thomas Jefferson, son of Randolph's daughter Jane and Colonel Peter Jefferson.

John RANDOLPH, 1728-1784

The son of Sir John Randolph and nephew of Isham, John Randolph was the author of a *Treatise on Gardening*, the first American book on kitchen gardening. Previously only books written for the English climate had been available.

Lady SKIPWITH, ——-1826

Jean Miller, the daughter of a Scottish merchant, married Sir Peyton Skipwith of Prestwould, a plantation on the Dan River. Her brother-in-law, Colonel Henry Skipwith, owned the George Wythe House in Williamsburg toward the end of the century. Lady Skipwith's "Garden Notes" of 1793 are a valuable, if slight, addition to Virginian records.

George WASHINGTON, 1732-1799

Washington was greatly interested in horticulture and in scientific agriculture. As a member of the House of Burgesses he visited Williamsburg frequently and in 1759 married Martha Dandridge, widow of Daniel Parke Custis, son of John Custis of Williamsburg.

References to the Text

Page 8. Kalm's remarks on the popularity of life everlasting are from *Travels into North America*, Vol. I, pp. 130-31.

Page 12. Catesby recorded in his *Natural History*, Vol. I, p. xxii, seeing pomegranates "in great perfection in the Gardens of the Hon. *William Byrd*, Esq.; in the freshes of *James* river in *Virginia*." On September 20, 1711, Byrd noted in his diary sending four pomegranates grown at Westover to the governor. Several pages in his *Natural History of Virginia* are devoted to "Trees, Which Are Cultivated, and Grow in the Orchards, Which One Has Brought There From England and Other Places." See pp. 43-47 of the 1940 edition.

Page 13. Information on the methods employed in the eighteenth century to preserve fruits and flowers and to force them may be found in Hill's *Eden*. Miller's remarks on everlastings are from *Figures of Plants*, Vol. II, p. 186.

Page 14. "Prickly Lantana (house plant) very Brilliant, seldom without flowers." "Cyclamen . . . Blows in Decr. and continues in beauty till late in Spring." See *Garden Gossip*, Vol. X (1935), No. 4, p. 3.

Page 16. For historical references to the poet's narcissus see *Eden*, pp. 495-96. The Collinson-Bartram exchange on the double white daffodil may be found in Darlington, *Memorials of John Bartram and Humphry Marshall*, pp. 252, 255, 260.

Page 17. For Hill's description of the hyacinth, see *Eden*, p. 392.

Pages 18-19. Catesby mentions the atamasco lily in his *Natural History*, Vol. II, p. 112 and the Collinson letter is recorded in *Memorials of John Bartram*, p. 135.

Page 19. In 1737 Collinson wrote Bartram of the lilac, "As your neighbours of Virginia, in particular Colonel CUSTIS at Williamsburgh, who has undoubtedly the best collection in that country, desired some, I thought possibly you might want them." *Memorials of John Bartram*, p. 108.

Page 20. Miller describes the sweet William in his *Gardeners Dictionary*, Vol. I, under *Caryophyllus barbatus*. (Unfortunately the *Dictionary* is unpaged. Entries, however, are alphabetically arranged.)

Page 21. For descriptions of the chimney flower, see the *Gardeners Dictionary*, Vol. I, under *Campanula pyramidata*, and Loudon's *Encyclopædia*, p. 989. Hill's comments on the peony are quoted from *Eden*, p. 451.

Page 22. Miller's remarks on monkshood are from the *Gardeners Dictionary*, Vol. I, under *Aconitum*.

Page 23. Charles Evelyn, *The Lady's Recreation*, p. 25.

Page 26. Collinson's letter is from *Memorials of John Bartram*, p. 223.

Page 28. Both Hill quotations are from *Eden*, pp. 654 and 607 respectively.

Page 31. Gardeners Dictionary, Vol. I, under *Punica*.

Page 33. Evelyn, who dubbed the tulip "Glory of the Spring," called the carnation "Pride of Summer." *The Lady's Recreation*, p. 25.

Pages 34-35. Dr. Galt's letter is re-printed in *Tyler's Quarterly*, Vol. II, No. 4, pp. 246-47.

Page 37. For Hill's full description of gladioli see *Eden*, pp. 498-99. Furber mentions the double nasturtium, "esteem'd as a great Rarity," in *The Flower-Garden Display'd*, p. 58, and Randolph's evaluation may be found in *A Treatise on Gardening*, p. 74. The story of the hoarded tuberose is from Miller's *Gardeners Dictionary*, Vol. I, under *Hyacinthus Tuberosus*.

Pages 37-38. The Custis-Collinson letters on the tuberose are quoted, by permission of the American Antiquarian Society, from *Brothers of the Spade* pp. 50, 64, 82.

Page 39. On China asters, see *Memorials of John Bartram*, p. 67, and *Eden*, p. 649.

Page 40. Information on the important place given both goldenrod and asters is to be found in Miller's *Gardeners Dictionary*, Vol. I, under *Virga Aurea* and *Aster*.

Page 41. The American Gardener, Chapter VI, paragraphs 330-31.

Page 42. On "naked ladies" see *Garden Gossip*, Vol. X (1935), No. 4, p. 3 and the Pierpont Morgan Library catalogue, *Flowers of Ten Centuries*, p. 22.

Page 44. "Great quantities of tropical fruit, which, from the short run between Jamaica and New York, were there almost as plenty and cheap, as in their native soil." [Anne] Grant, *Memoirs of an American Lady . . . Previous to the Revolution* (London, 1809), p. 313.

Page 45. Collinson's letter on the pomegranate is from *Memorials of John Bartram*, p. 244. See *Eden*, pp. 19-20, for Hill's full description of this fruit. Kalm remarks on the eighteenth-century method of preserving melons in *Travels into North America*, Vol. III, p. 264.

Page 46. Hill's excellent advice is from *Eden*, p. 22.

Page 49. From the *Gardeners Dictionary*, Vol. I, under *Amaranthoides*.

Page 51. "Purple cuped Statice or Thrift, dried it retains its colour which renders it ornamental for a Mantelpiece in Winter." "Garden Notes," *Garden Gossip*, Vol. X (1935), no. 4, p. 3. For the colors of strawflowers, see *Figures of Plants*, Vol. II, p. 186, already quoted. Collinson's letter to Custis is from *Brothers of the Spade*, p. 100, and is quoted by permission of the publishers.

Page 52. See *Travels into North America*, Vol. I, pp. 130-31, already quoted.

Page 57. See note to page 14.

Pages 58-78. In addition to the works listed in the bibliographical note, I have relied for biographical details on information compiled by the Research Department of Colonial Williamsburg and on such standard works as the *Encyclopædia Britannica*, the *Dictionary of American Biography*, the *Encyclopedia of Virginia Biography*, and the *Dictionary of National Biography*.

Page 65. Bartram's letter is quoted from *Memorials of John Bartram*, p. 120. E. G. Swem quotes Collinson to this effect in *Brothers of the Spade*, p. 19, and I have requoted by permission.

Page 67. Mrs. Logan's letter to Bartram will be found in *Memorials of John Bartram*, p. 414.

Page 71. Jefferson's tribute to Clayton is from his *Notes on the State of Virginia* (Philadelphia, 1825), p. 57.

Page 72. Bartram's evaluation of the Clayton and Custis gardens is contained in a letter from Collinson to Custis reprinted in *Brothers of the Spade*, p. 80.

Pages 72-73. Collinson's letter on the "Mule" is quoted from *Memorials of John Bartram*, p. 136.

Page 76. Bailey, quoting Ramsay, describes Mrs. Logan thus in his *Cyclopedia*, Vol. II, p. 1510.

A Note to the Curious

THE most fascinating reading I did in connection with my research on eighteenth-century plant materials and flower arrangements was in three contemporary sources, John Hill, *Eden* (London, 1757), Philip Miller, *The Gardeners Dictionary* (2 v., London, 1737-1739), and his beautifully illustrated supplementary volumes *Figures of the Most Beautiful, Useful, and Uncommon Plants Described in the Gardeners Dictionary* (2 v., London, 1771). I also thoroughly enjoyed, and highly recommend, Charles Evelyn, *The Lady's Recreation* (London, 1717). All four, unfortunately, are rarities, but the general reader does have access to other delightful contemporary accounts. Much of the correspondence between John Bartram and Peter Collinson is available in William Darlington, *Memorials of John Bartram and Humphry Marshall* (Philadelphia, 1849), and *Brothers of the Spade,* ably edited and annotated by the dean of Virginia historians, Dr. E. G. Swem (Worcester,

Mass., 1949) is a collection of the letters of Peter Collinson and Williamsburg's own John Custis.

Several travel accounts I found particularly rewarding are also difficult to obtain except through large libraries: John Lawson, *A New Voyage to Carolina* (London, 1709), Peter Kalm, *Travels into North America* (3 v., Warrington and London, 1770-71), and Andrew Burnaby, *Travels Through the Middle Settlements of North America ... 1759 and 1760* (London, 1798). However, William Bartram's travel accounts were recently edited by Mark Van Doren as *The Travels of William Bartram* (New York, 1940) and Ernest Earnest, *John and William Bartram: Botanists and Explorers* (Philadelphia, 1940), R. Hingston Fox, *Dr. John Fothergill and His Friends* (London, 1919), and Howard A. Kelly, *Some American Medical Botanists* (Troy, N.Y., 1914, reprinted New York, 1929) make excellent supplementary reading.

I have already acknowledged my debt

to the Kensington gardener, Robert Furber, whose *The Flower-Garden Display'd* (London, 1732) contains in book form reproductions of and commentary on the famous flower prints which he first published in 1730. I should also like to call attention to two modern volumes which I consult constantly: Ralph Warner, *Dutch and Flemish Flower and Fruit Painters of the XVIIth and XVIIIth Centuries* (London, 1928), and Gordon Dunthorne, *Flower and Fruit Prints of the 18th and Early 19th Centuries* (Washington, 1938). Kate Doggett Boggs, "Notes on Old Floral Decoration" (*The National Horticultural Magazine,* October, 1936, pp. 223-44) contains useful information on eighteenth-century containers.

It would be fruitless to list here all the sources I consulted in my research on the authenticity of plant materials, for only the specialist would find the complete list useful. It is perhaps proper, however, to record those I found particularly helpful. Among seventeenth- and eighteenth-century botanical works, in addition to Philip Miller and John Hill already cited, Richard Bradley, *Dictionarium Botanicum* (2 v., London, 1728), William Byrd, *Natural History of Virginia* (available in a modern printing, Richmond, 1940), Mark

Catesby, *The Natural History of Carolina, Florida, and the Bahama Islands* (2 v., London, 1771), John Josselyn, *New Englands Rarities Discovered* (London, 1672), Thomas Mawe and John Abercrombie, *Every Man his own Gardener* (London, 1782), John Spurrier, *The Practical Farmer* (Wilmington, Del., 1793), Benjamin Townsend, *The Complete Seedsman* (London, 1726), and Thomas Walter, *Flora Caroliniana* (London, 1788) occur again and again in my notes. Worth separate mention is the record of John Clayton's indefatigable labors in the Virginia Tidewater and Piedmont, published under the name of its European compiler, J. F. Gronovius, as *Flora Virginica* (Leyden, 1743). Bernard MacMahon, *American Gardener's Calendar* (Philadelphia, 1806) and William Cobbett, *The American Gardener* (London, 1821) are interesting historically and J. C. Loudon, *An Encyclopædia of Gardening* (London, 1822) and Sir Joseph Paxton, *Paxton's Botanical Dictionary* (London, 1868) are valuable nineteenth-century botanical dictionaries. Foremost among modern reference works is L. H. Bailey, *The Standard Cyclopedia of Horticulture* (3 v., New York, 1941), an indispensable aid in matching our present flower varieties with the varieties known, often by another name, to the colonists. Alfred Rehder, *Manual of Cultivated Trees and Shrubs* (New York, 1937), *Standardized Plant Names* (Harrisburg, Pa., 1942), L. H. Bailey, *Manual of Cultivated Plants* (New York, 1949), and M. L. Fernald, editor, *Gray's Manual of Botany* (8th edition, New York, 1950) were also consulted on identification and nomenclature.

A search through contemporary newspaper advertisements, especially the Boston *Evening Post* and the Maryland and Virginia *Gazettes*, yielded firsthand information on the availability of plant materials. Also valuable as sources for authenticity, and engrossing in themselves, are the writings of and about amateur horticulturists: *Thomas Jefferson's Garden Book, 1766-1824*, annotated by E. M. Betts (Philadelphia, 1944), Lady Skipwith's "Garden Notes" (published in *Garden Gossip*, X, 1935: number 2, pp. 9-10, number 4, pp. 3-4, and number 6, pp. 3-4), R. L. Stoddert, "A Seed List of 1798" (also published in *Garden Gossip*, VII, 1932, p. 14), and John Randolph, Jr., *A Treatise on Gardening* (Richmond, 1929) are particularly valuable in that they were written by eighteenth-century Virginians about Virginia gardens. Both *The*

Secret Diary of William Byrd of Westover, 1709-1712 edited by Louis B. Wright and Marion Tinling (Richmond, 1941) and *The Diaries of George Washington, 1748-1799*, edited by J. C. Fitzpatrick (4 v., Boston, 1925) contain many references to specific plants, although not in such accessible form as the others. E. M. Betts and H. B. Perkins, *Thomas Jefferson's Flower Garden at Monticello* (Richmond, 1941), a short article by Mary F. Goodwin, "Three Eighteenth-Century Gardens" (*Virginia Quarterly Review*, April, 1934, pp. 218-33), and the more comprehensive "Colonial Gardens: The Landscape Architecture of George Washington's Time" in *History of the George Washington Bicentennial Celebration* (Washington, 1932) are also recommended for further reading.

A good contemporary account dealing with the over-all picture of gardening in former days is contained in Stephen Switzer, *Ichnographia Rustica: or, The Nobleman, Gentleman, and Gardener's Recreation* (3 v., London, 1742). Those interested in this broader phase will also find Richardson Wright, *The Story of Gardening* (New York, 1934) and *Gardens of Colony and State* edited by A. G. B. Lockwood (2 v., New York, 1934) well worth investigation.

Recent studies which contribute to the knowledge of eighteenth-century plant materials are the Pierpont Morgan Library exhibition catalogue, *Flowers of Ten Centuries* (New York, 1947) and E. H. Wilson's popular article "Plants of our Great-Grandmother's Day" (*House & Garden*, April, 1930, pp. 80-81, 164-170). In *The Flora of the Peninsula of Virginia* (reprinted from "Papers of the Michigan Academy of Science, Arts and Letters," 1924), E. W. Erlandson has written a scholarly study of the plants of this region.

The recommendations made here do not constitute a comprehensive bibliography of the field, but if the curious reader is tempted to further reading by this listing, I well know how great will be his discoveries and rewards.

Index to Plant Material

A list of flowers, fruits, and nuts
mentioned in the text with the species used in the arrangements
of Colonial Williamsburg shown in italics

This book has been set in Monotype Centaur Roman
and Arrighi Italic
It was designed, printed, and bound at
The Lakeside Press, R. R. Donnelley & Sons Company
Chicago, Illinois
Crawfordsville, Indiana